Easy Piano

Contemporary Christian Christmas

ISBN-13: 978-1-4234-1365-3
ISBN-10: 1-4234-1365-2

HAL•LEONARD®
CORPORATION

7777 W. BLUEMOUND RD. P.O. BOX 13819 MILWAUKEE, WI 53213

Visit Hal Leonard Online at
www.halleonard.com

BREATH OF HEAVEN
(Mary's Song)

Words and Music by AMY GRANT
and CHRIS EATON

won - der ___ what I've ___ done. ___ Ho - ly
world as ___ cold as ___ stone, ___ must I
of - fer ___ all I ___ am ___ for the

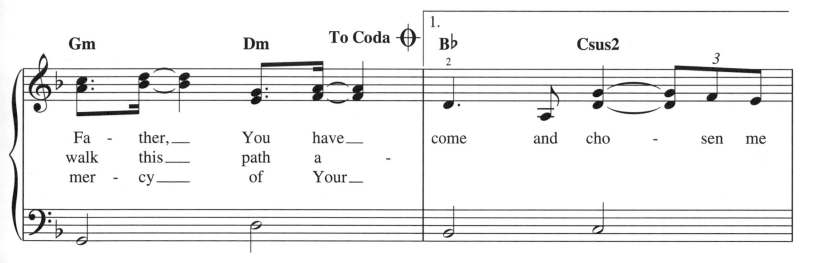

Fa - ther, ___ You have ___ come and cho - sen me
walk this ___ path a -
mer - cy ___ of Your ___

now ___ to car - ry Your Son. I am

lone? Be ___ with me now, ___ be ___ with me now.

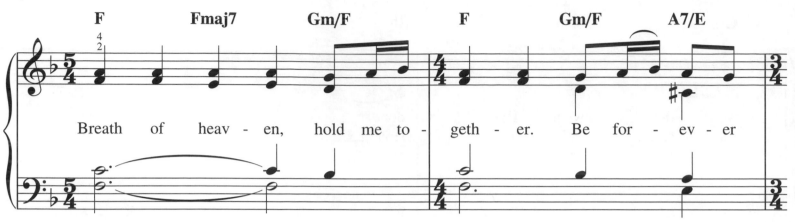

Breath of heav - en, hold me to - geth - er. Be for - ev - er

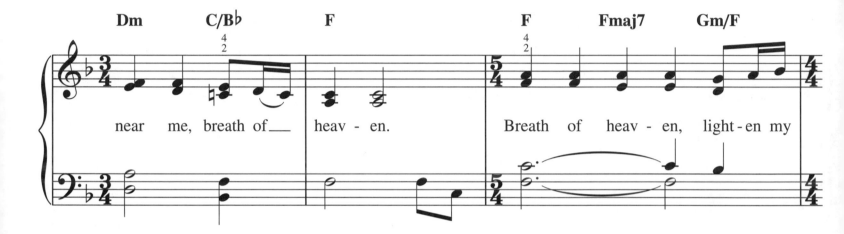

near me, breath of___ heav - en. Breath of heav - en, light - en my

dark - ness. Pour o - ver me Your ho - li - ness, for You are ho - ly,

D.S. al Coda

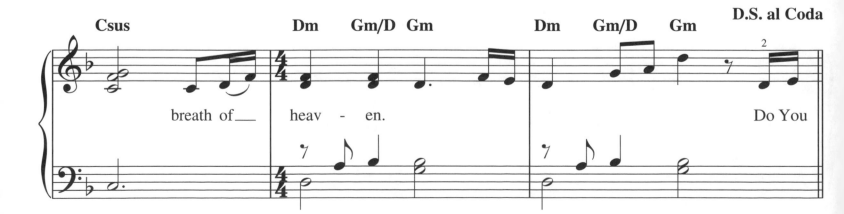

breath of___ heav - en. Do You

CODA

plan. Help me be strong, help me be....

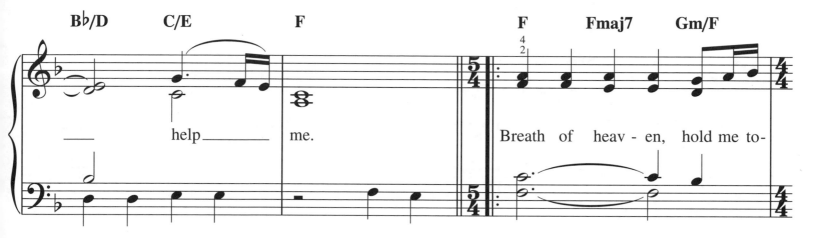

help me. Breath of heav - en, hold me to-

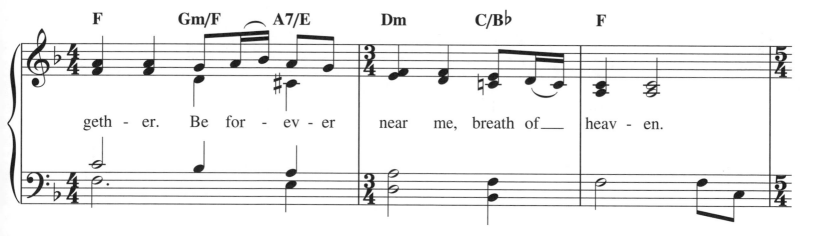

geth - er. Be for - ev - er near me, breath of heav - en.

Breath of heav - en, light - en my dark - ness. Pour o - ver me Your

6

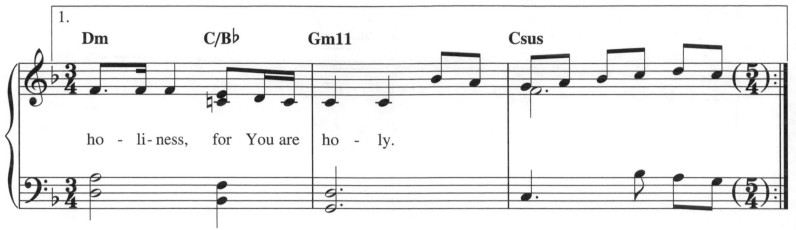

ho - li - ness, for You are ho - ly.

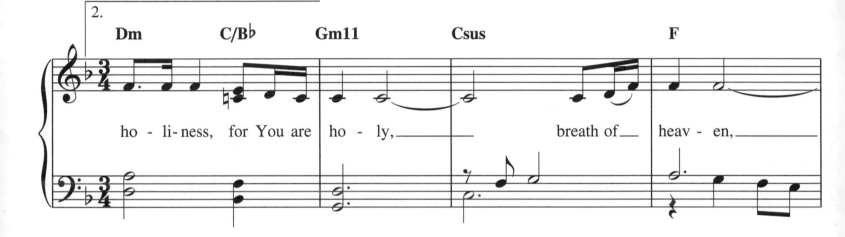

ho - li - ness, for You are ho - ly,_____ breath of__ heav - en,_____

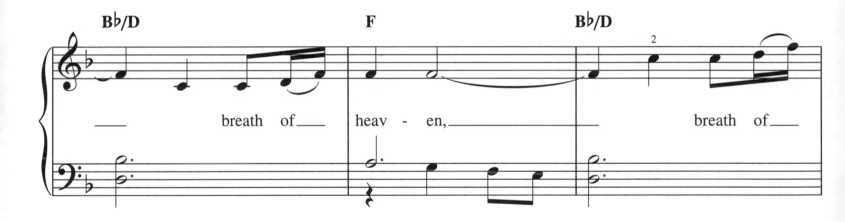

_____ breath of__ heav - en,_____ breath of__

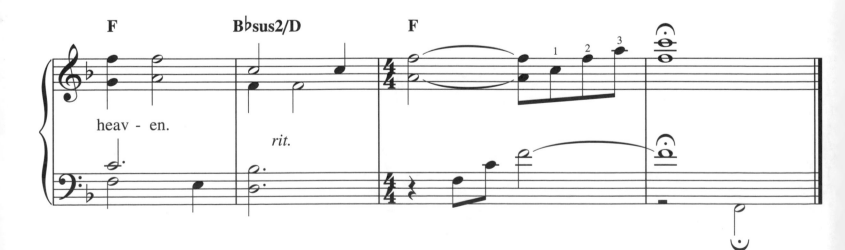

heav - en. *rit.*

CHILD OF LOVE

Words and Music by STEVE HINDALONG,
MARK D. LEE and MATTHEW WEST

Moderately slow, in 2

With pedal

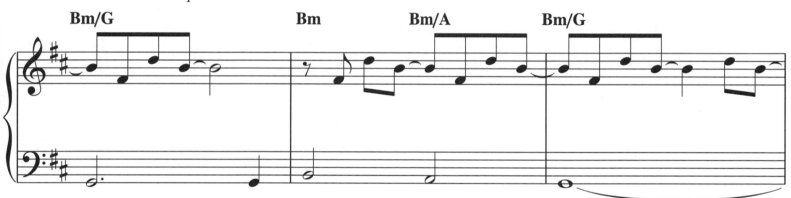

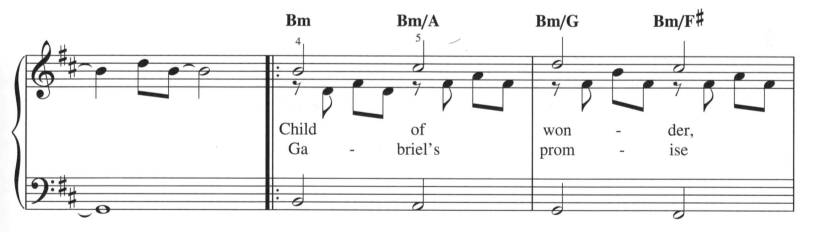

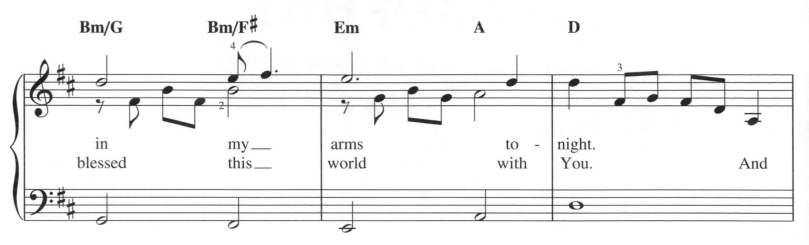

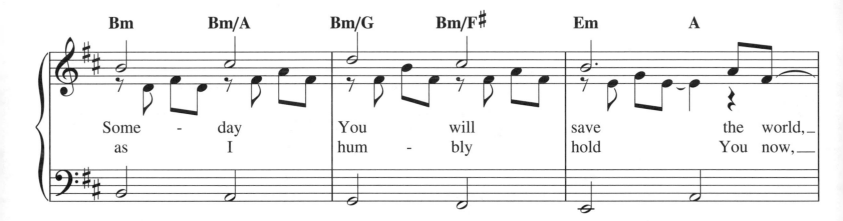

9

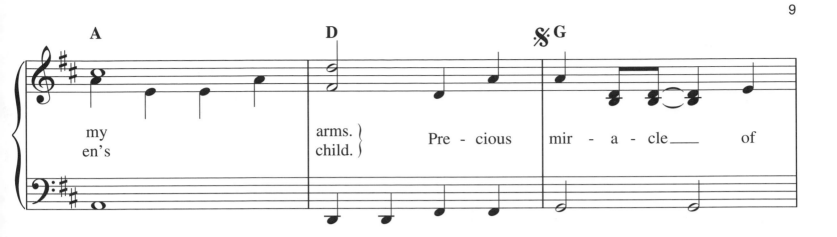

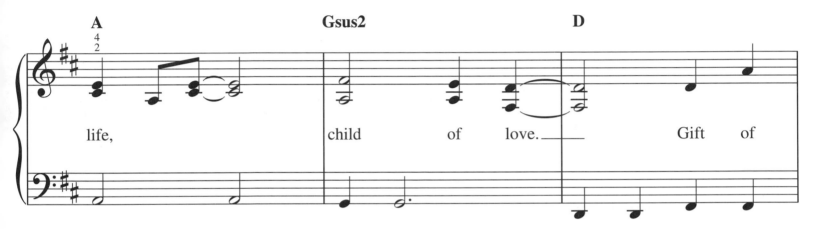

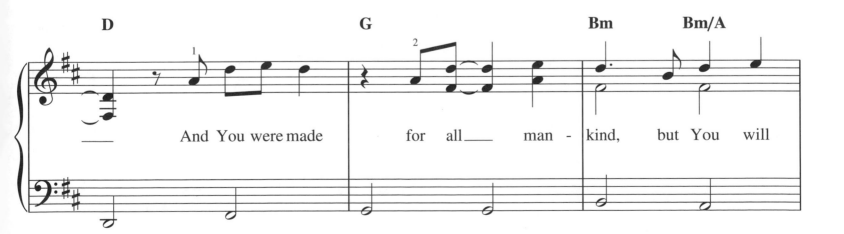

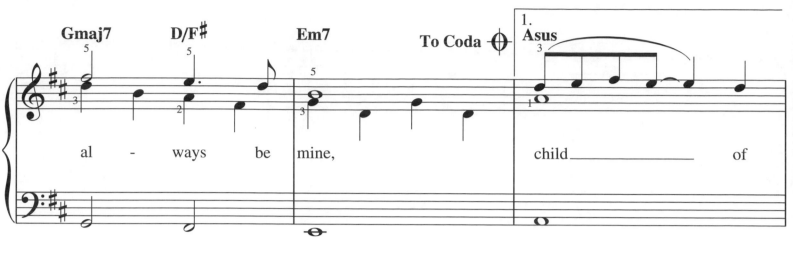

al - ways be mine, child_____ of

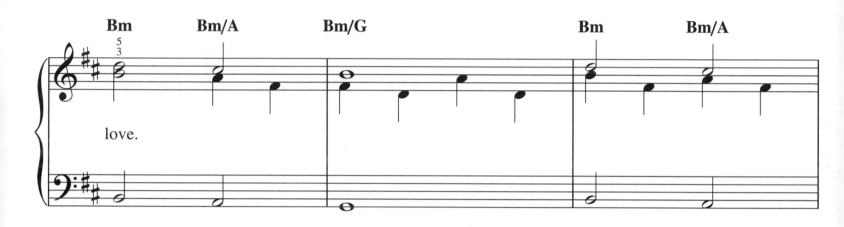

love.

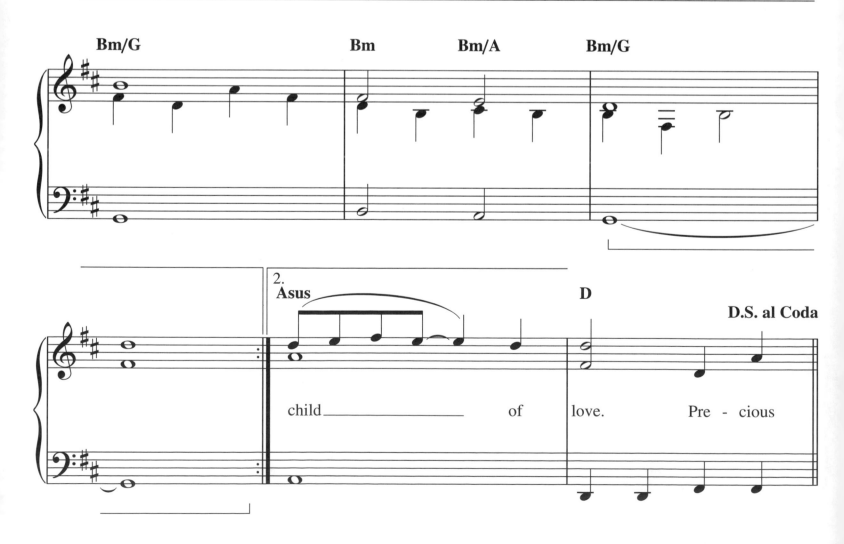

child_____ of love. Pre - cious

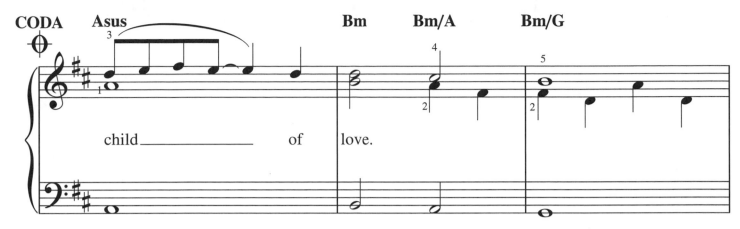

CODA

child _____ of love.

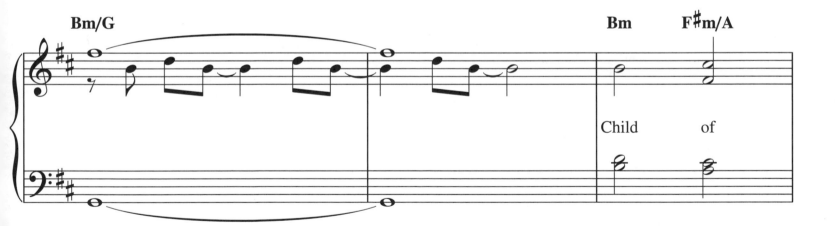

Child of

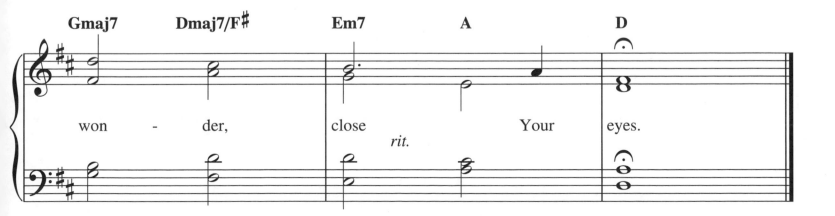

won - der, close Your eyes.

rit.

THE CHRISTMAS SHOES

Words and Music by LEONARD AHLSTROM
and EDDIE CARSWELL

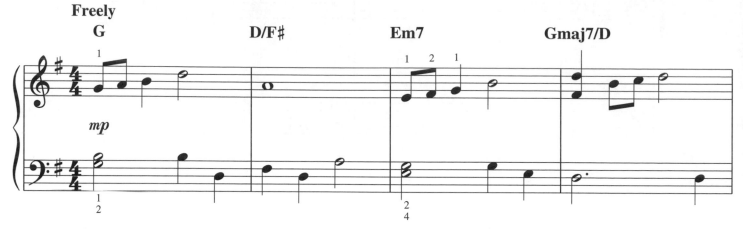

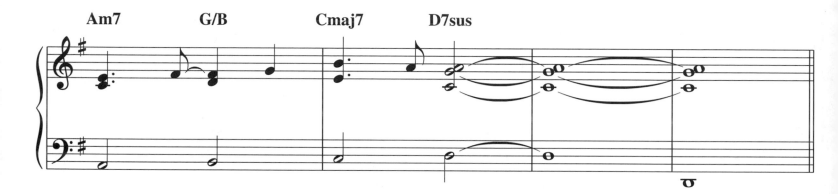

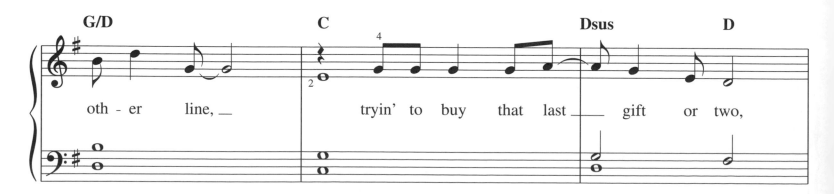

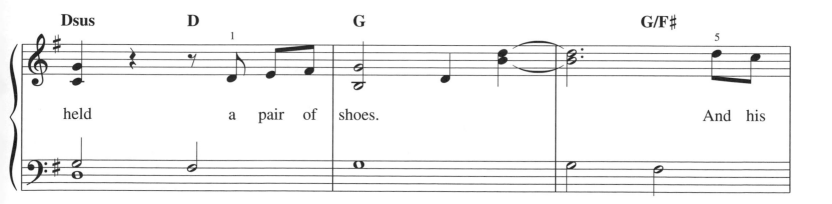

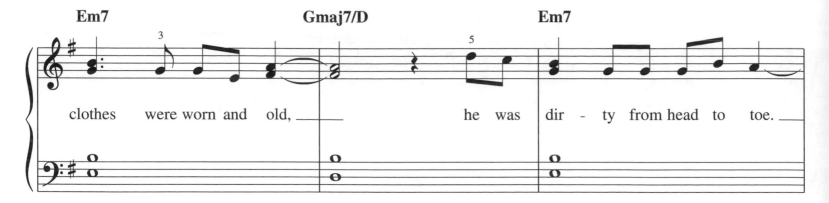

Em7   Gmaj7/D   Em7

clothes   were worn and   old, _____   he was   dir - ty from head to   toe.

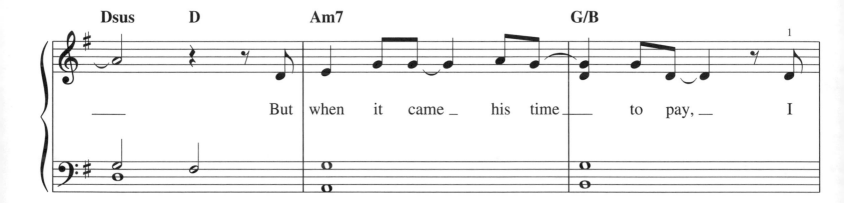

Dsus   D   Am7   G/B

_____   But   when   it   came _   his   time ___   to   pay, _   I

G/C   Dsus   D   **Chorus**

could-n't   be - lieve _   what I   heard   him say,   "Sir, I   wan - na

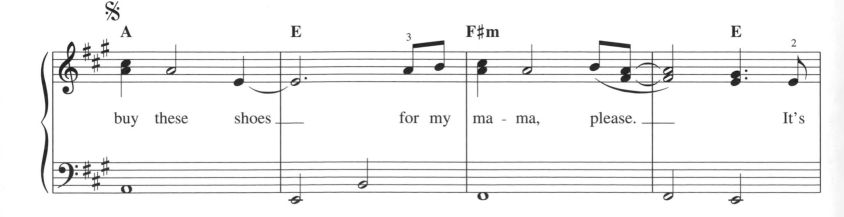

A   E   F#m   E

buy   these   shoes ___   for my   ma - ma,   please. ___   It's

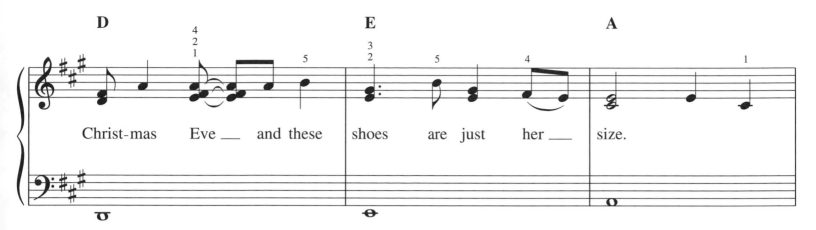

D **Esus** **E** **Bm7** **A/C♯**

want her to look beau - ti - ful ___ if Ma - ma ___ meets

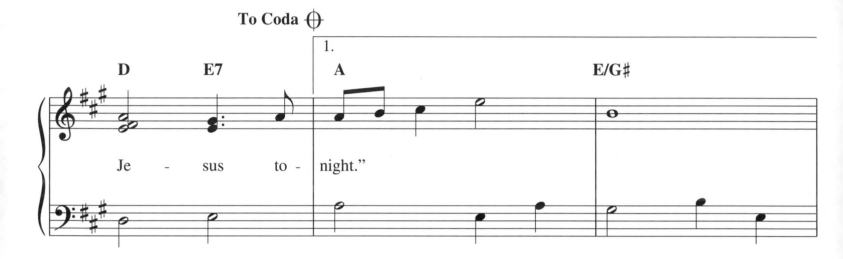

To Coda ⊕

1.

D **E7** **A** **E/G♯**

Je - sus to - night."

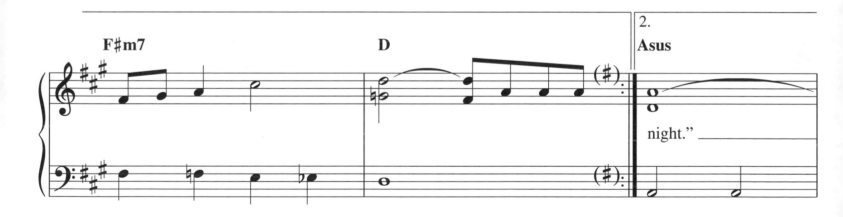

2.

F♯m7 **D** **Asus**

night." ___

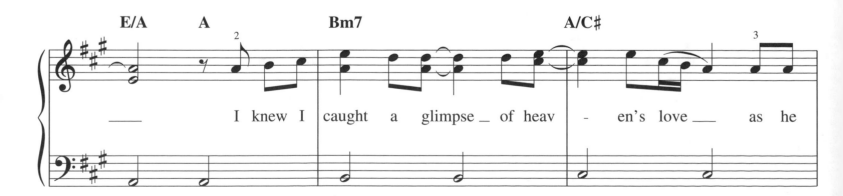

E/A **A** **Bm7** **A/C♯**

___ I knew I caught a glimpse ___ of heav - en's love ___ as he

17

thanked me and — ran out. — I knew that God had sent — that lit-

tle boy — to re - mind me ___ what

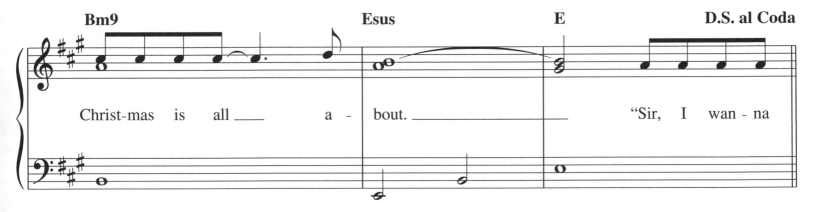

Christ-mas is all — a - bout. ___ "Sir, I wan - na

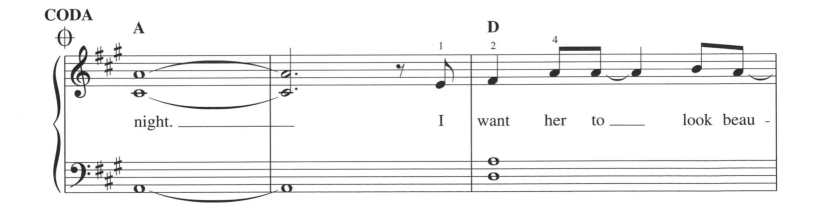

night. ___ I want her to — look beau -

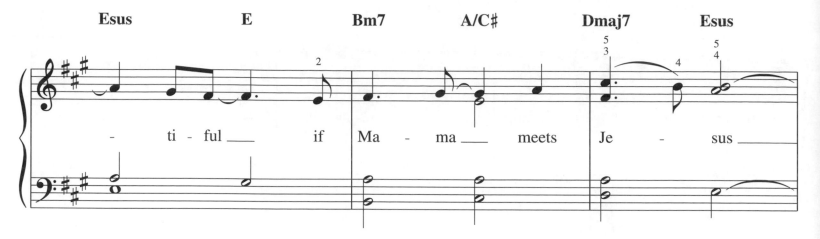

-ti-ful ___ if Ma - ma ___ meets Je - sus ___

___ to - night."

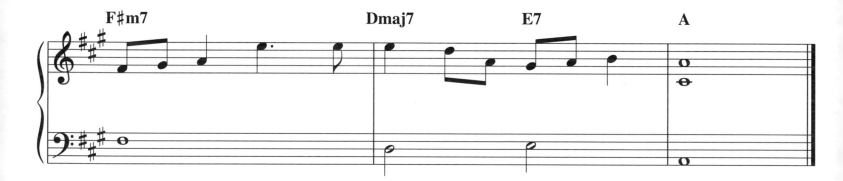

Additional Lyrics

2. They counted pennies for what seemed like years,
Then the cashier said, "Son, there's not enough here."
He searched his pockets frantic'lly,
Then he turned and he looked at me.
He said, "Mama made Christmas good at our house,
Though most years she just did without.
Tell me, sir, what am I gonna do?
Somehow I've gotta buy her these Christmas shoes."
So, I laid the money down,
I just had to help him out.
And I'll never forget the look on his face when he said,
"Mama's gonna look so great."
Chorus

CHRISTMASTIME

Words and Music by MICHAEL W. SMITH
and JOANNA CARLSON

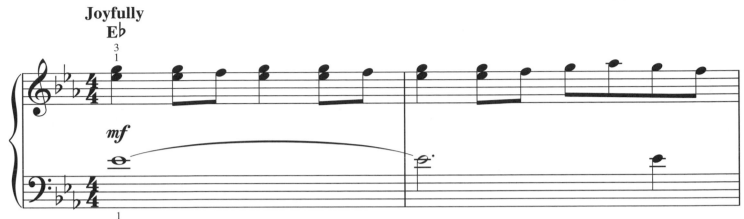

Ring Christ-mas bells, ring them loud with a mes-sage bring-ing

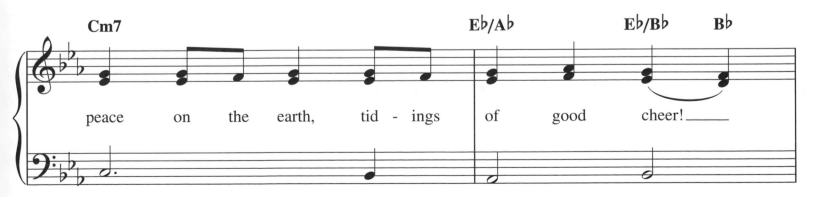

peace on the earth, tid-ings of good cheer!

Come, car - ol - ers, come and join with the an - gels sing - ing,

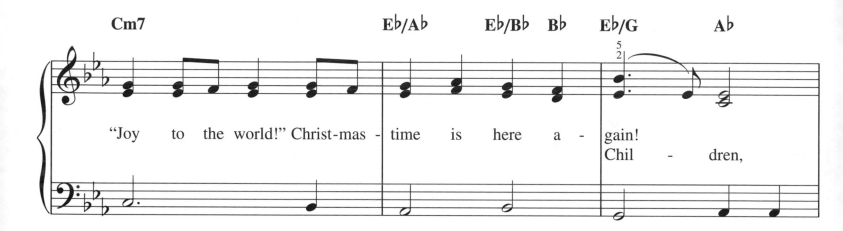

"Joy to the world!" Christ-mas - time is here a - gain!
Chil - dren,

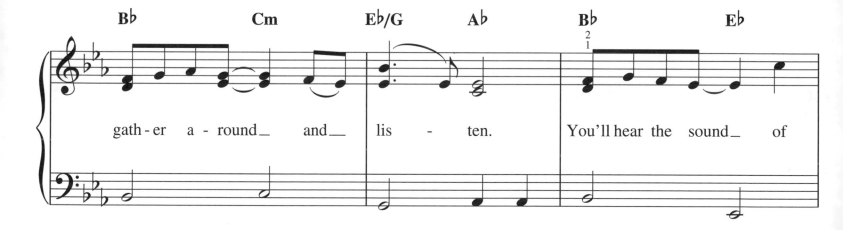

gath - er a - round__ and__ lis - ten. You'll hear the sound__ of

an - gels fill - ing the sky,__ tell - ing ev - 'ry - one

Christ - mas - time is _____ here! Ring Christ - mas bells, ring them

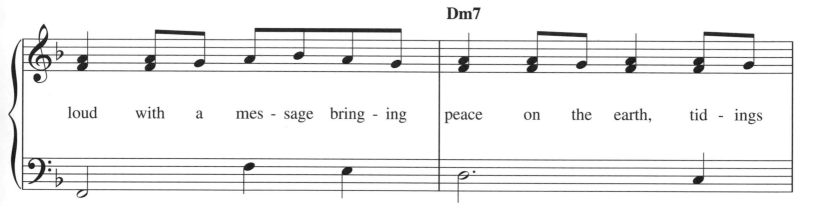

loud with a mes - sage bring - ing peace on the earth, tid - ings

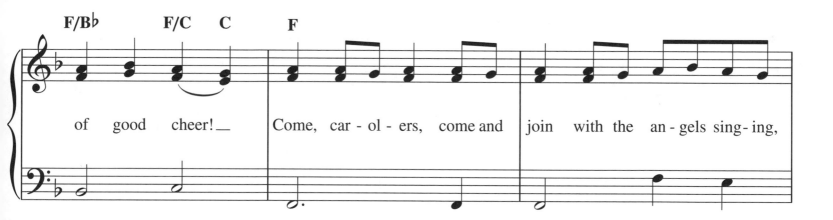

of good cheer! __ Come, car - ol - ers, come and join with the an - gels sing - ing,

"Joy to the world!" Christ-mas - time is here a - gain!
Loved _____ ones

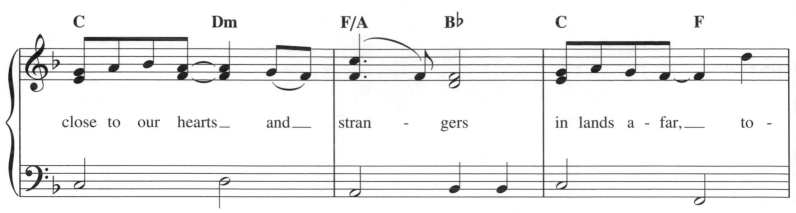

close to our hearts__ and__ stran - gers in lands a - far,__ to -

geth - er shar - ing the joy.__ Em - man - u - el. (Go

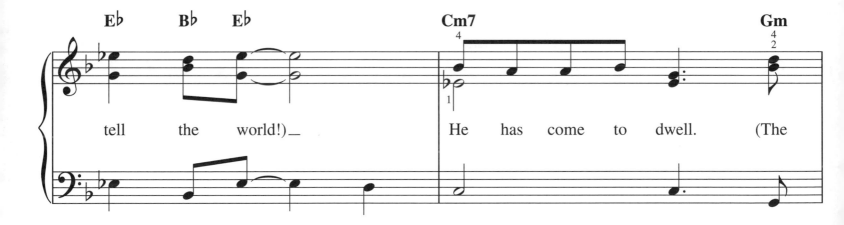

tell the world!)__ He has come to dwell. (The

time is near!)__ With__ one__ voice, let the world re -

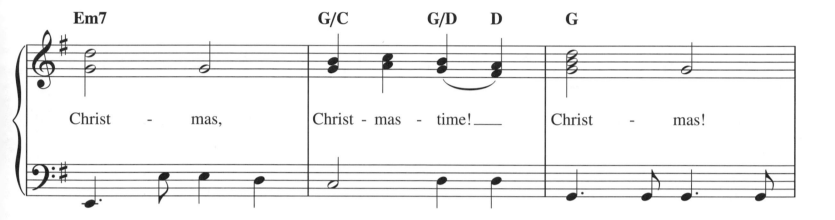

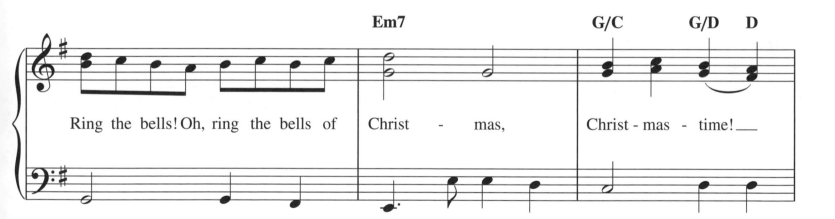

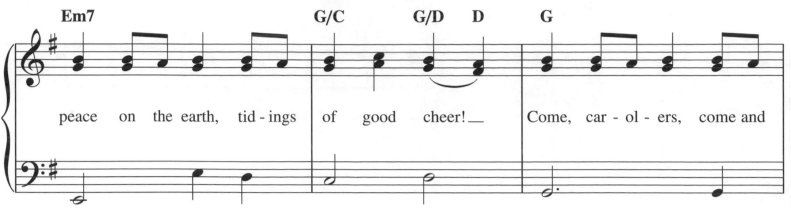

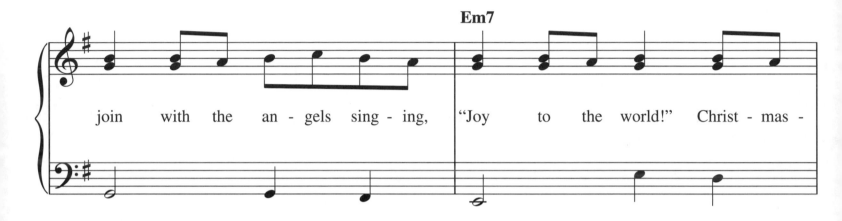

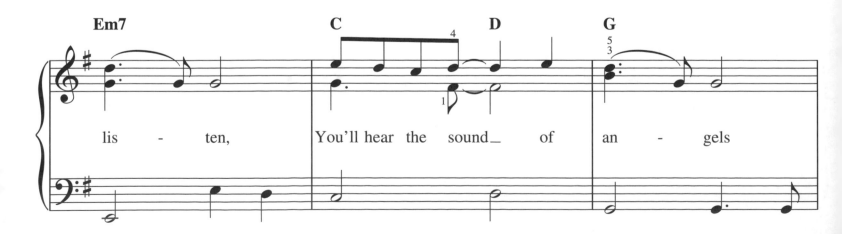

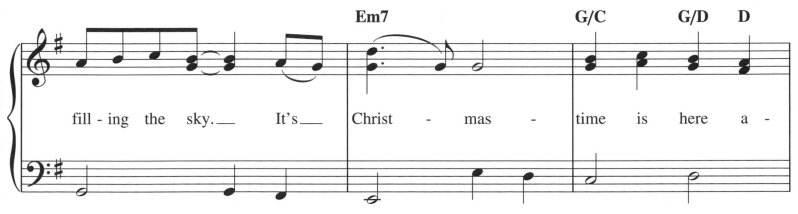

fill - ing the sky.___ It's___ Christ - mas - time is here a -

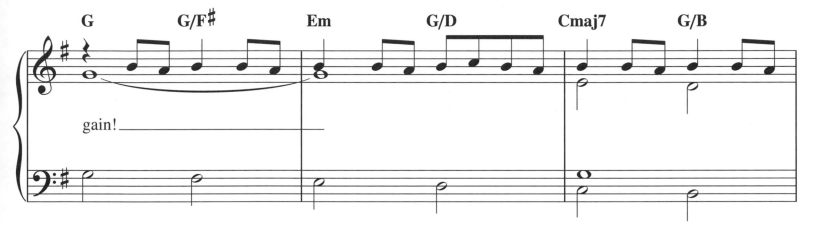

gain! _____

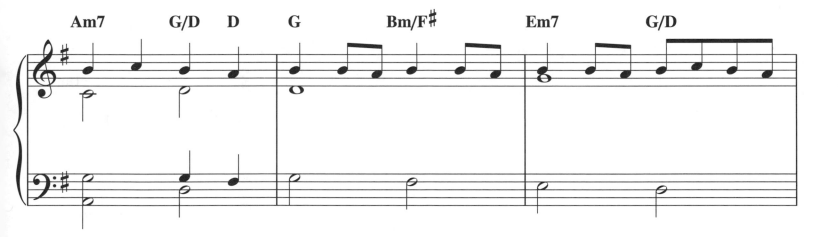

rit.

EMMANUEL

Words and Music by
MICHAEL W. SMITH

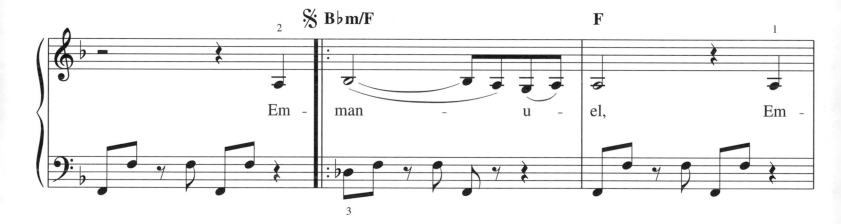

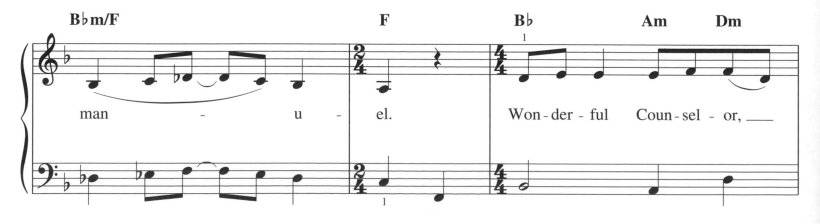

Lord of life, Lord of all, _____ He's _ the

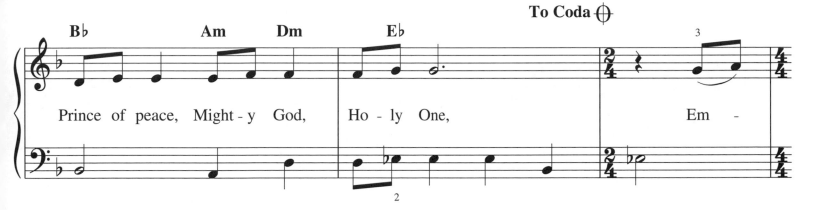

To Coda ⊕

Prince of peace, Might-y God, Ho-ly One, Em -

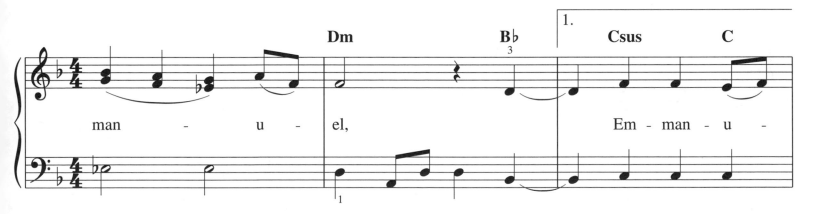

man - u - el, Em - man - u -

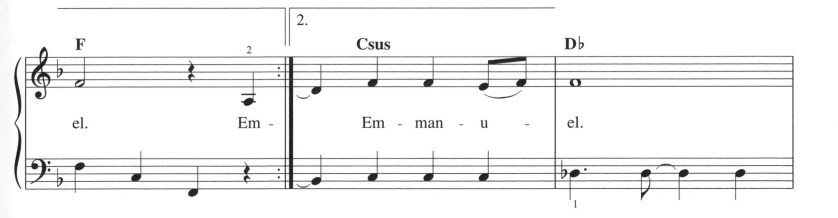

el. Em - Em - man - u - el.

D.S. al Coda

CODA

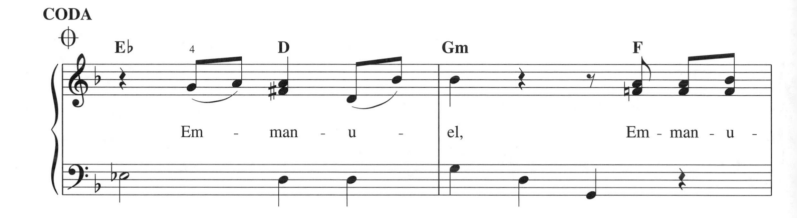

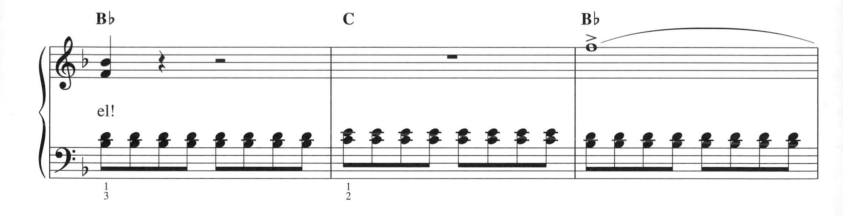

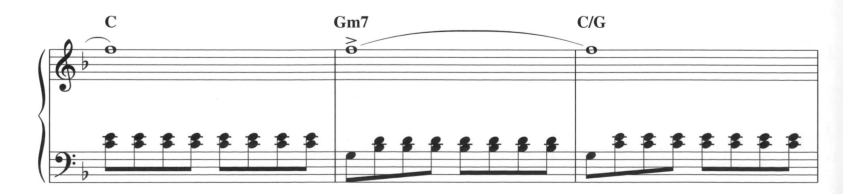

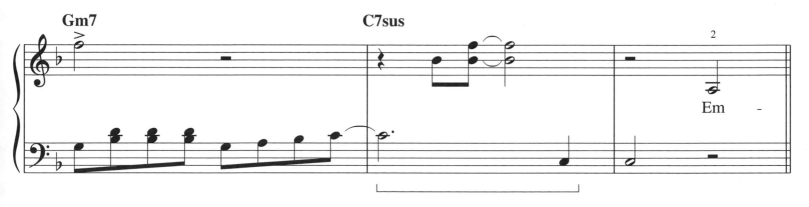

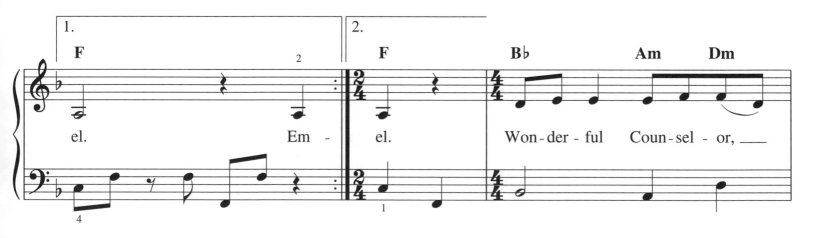

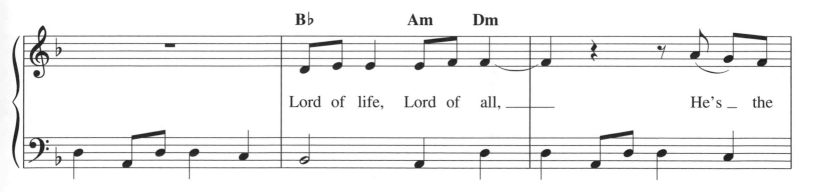

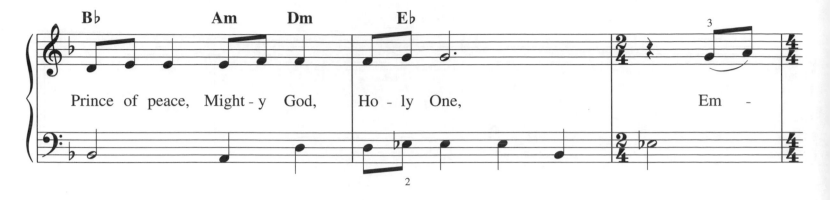

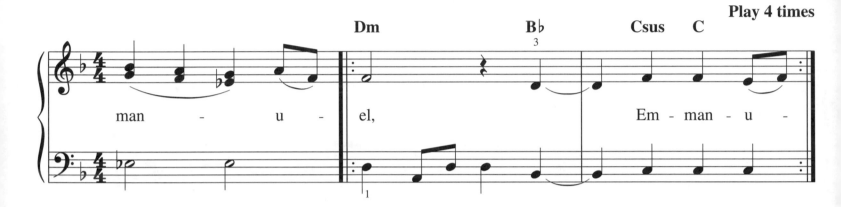

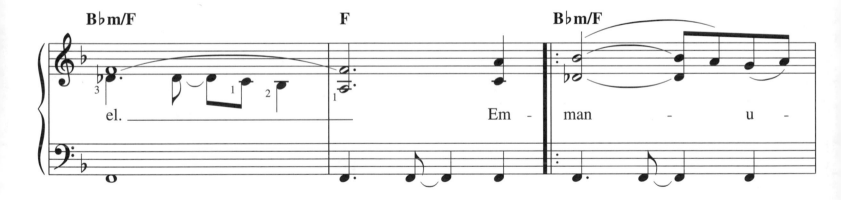

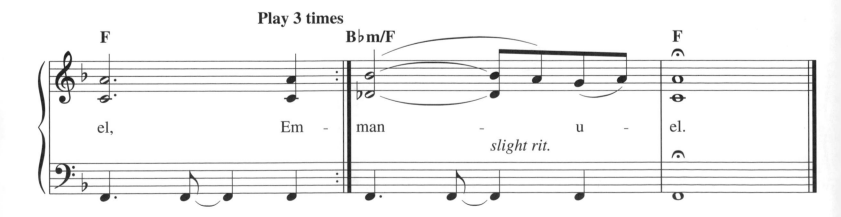

JESUS BORN ON THIS DAY

Words and Music by MARIAH CAREY
and WALTER AFANASIEFF

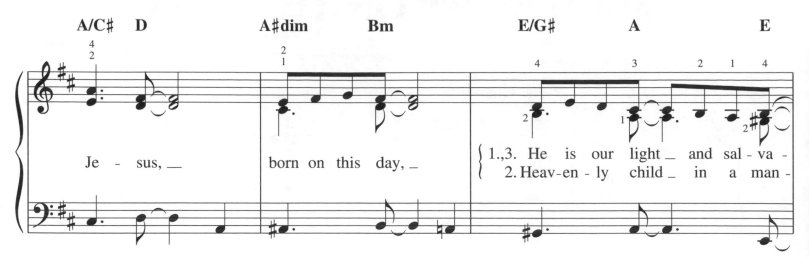

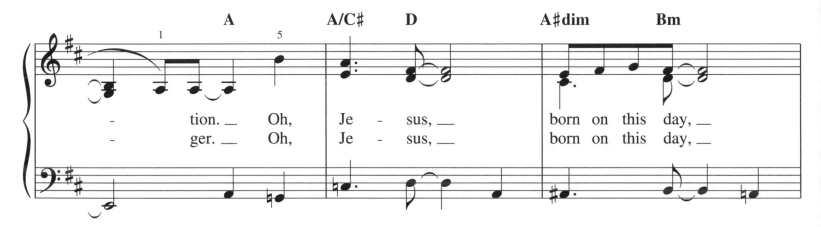

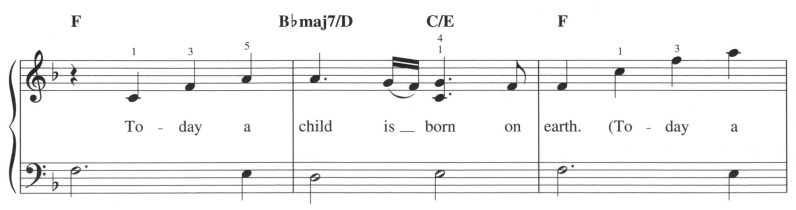

child   is _ born   on   earth.) He is light,   He is love,   He is grace,   born on Christ-mas

day. He is light,   He is love,   He is grace,   born on Christ-mas

1.

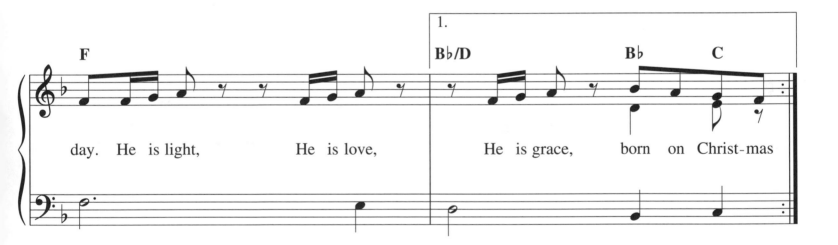

day. He is light,   He is love,   He is grace,   born on Christ-mas

2.

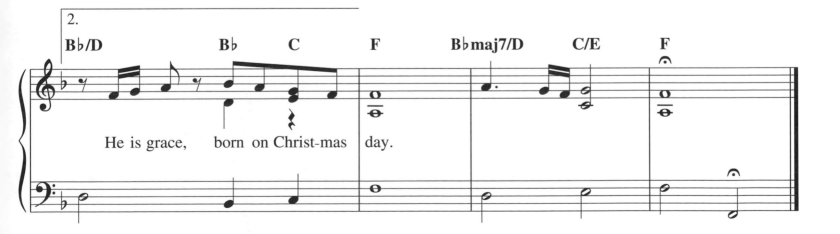

He is grace,   born on Christ-mas day.

HERE WITH US

Words and Music by JOY ELIZABETH WILLIAMS,
BEN GLOVER and JASON D. INGRAM

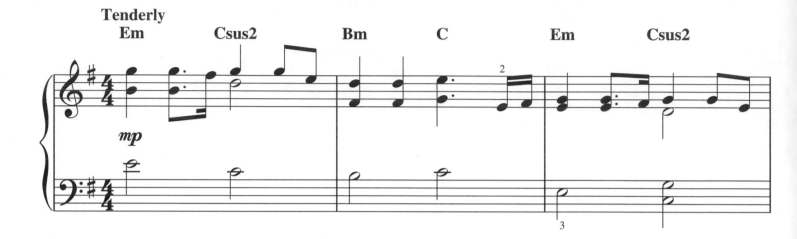

It's still a mys-ter-y___ to me

that the hands of God___ could be so small,___

how ti-ny fin-gers reach - ing in the night

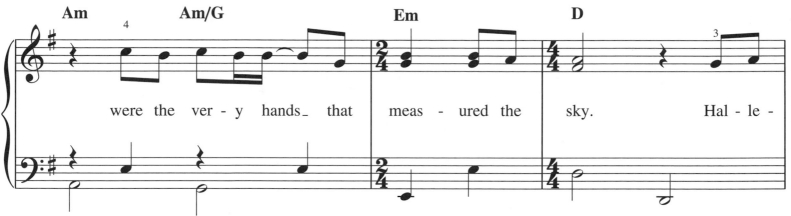

were the ver - y hands_ that meas - ured the sky. Hal - le -

lu - jah, hal - le - lu - jah! Heav - en's love reach-ing down to save the

world._____ Hal - le - lu - jah, hal - le - lu - jah! Son of

God, ser - vant King, here with us,_____ You're here with us.

Mmm. Still a mys-ter-y to me, oh,

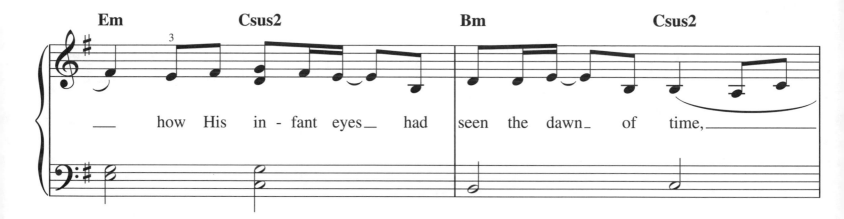

how His in-fant eyes had seen the dawn of time,

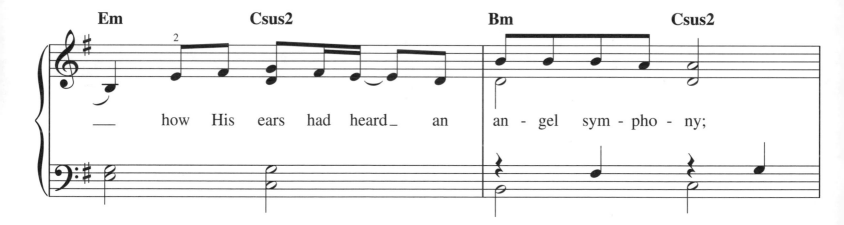

how His ears had heard an an-gel sym-pho-ny;

D.S. al Coda

but still, Mar-y had to rock her Sav-ior to sleep. Hal-le-

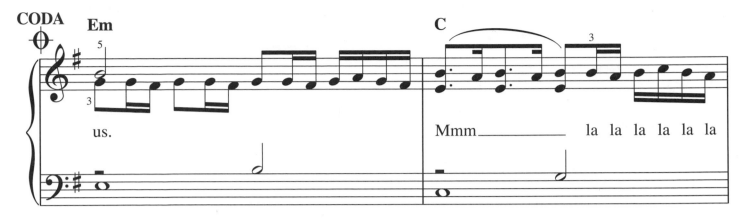

us.

Mmm_____ la la la la la la

la.

Oh._____

You're here.__

__

La la la la la la la la la la la la la la la la

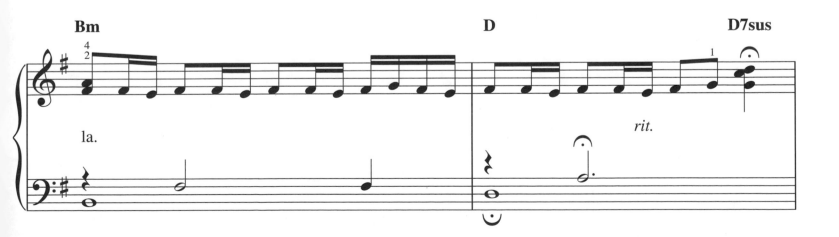

la.

rit.

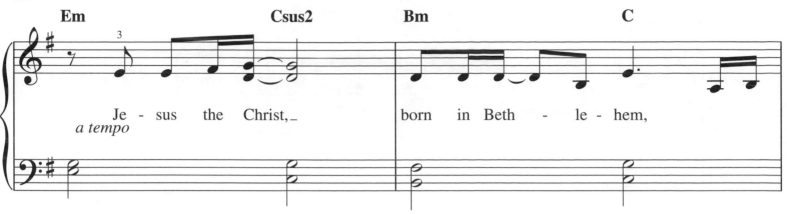

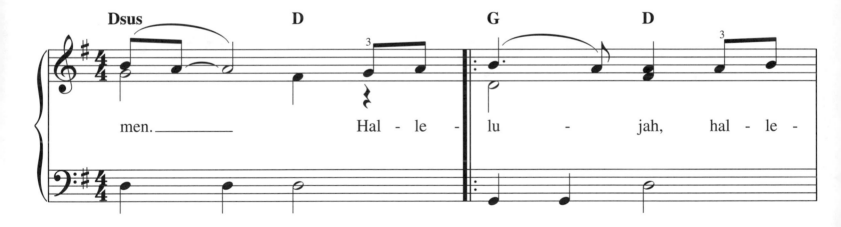

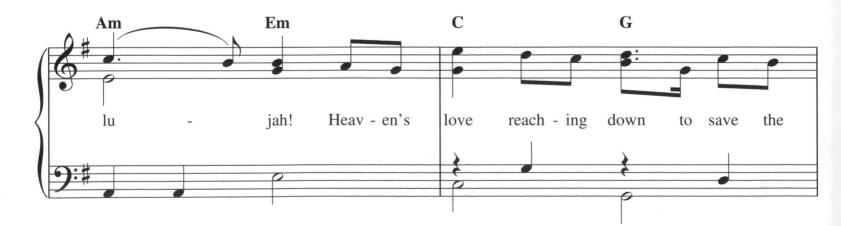

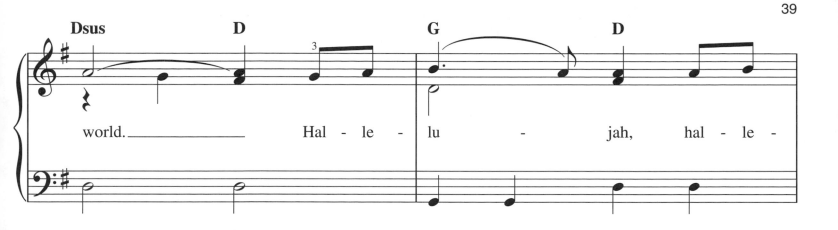

world._____ Hal - le - lu - jah, hal - le -

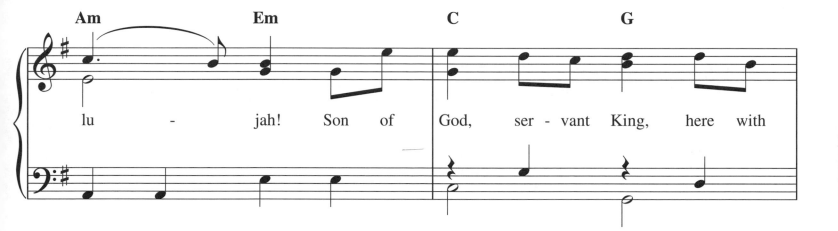

lu - jah! Son of God, ser - vant King, here with

us._____ Oh, hal - le - us,_____ You're here with us.

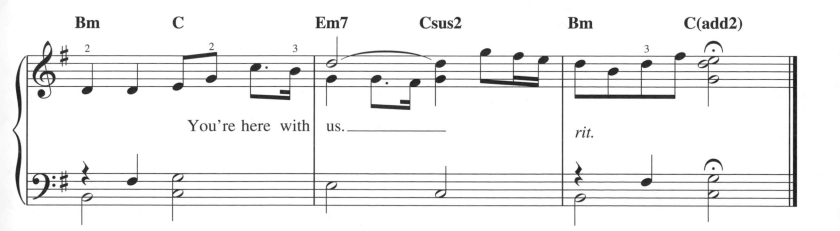

You're here with us._____ rit.

JOSEPH'S LULLABY

Words and Music by BART MILLARD
and BROWN BANNISTER

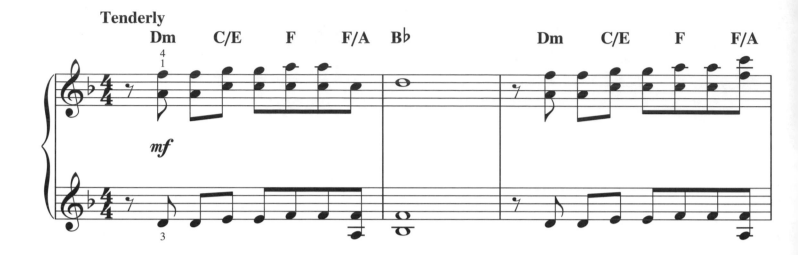

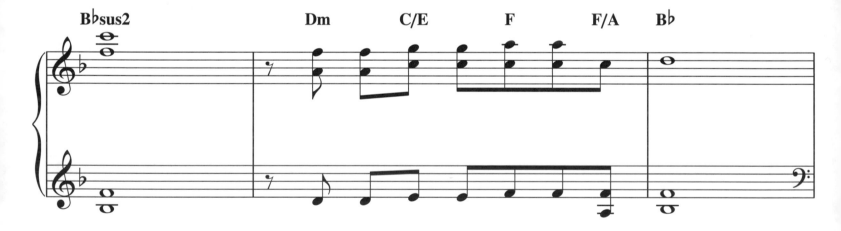

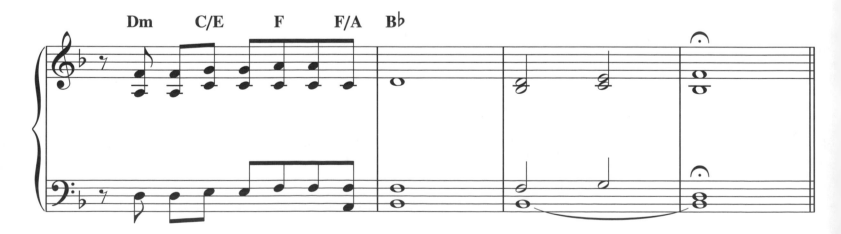

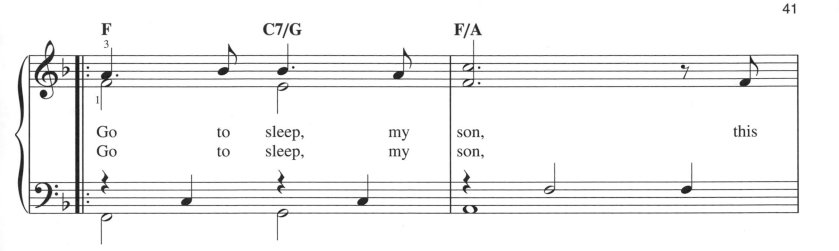

Go   to   sleep,   my   son,   this
Go   to   sleep,   my   son,

man - ger   for_____   Your   bed.   You
go   and   chase_____   Your   dreams.   This

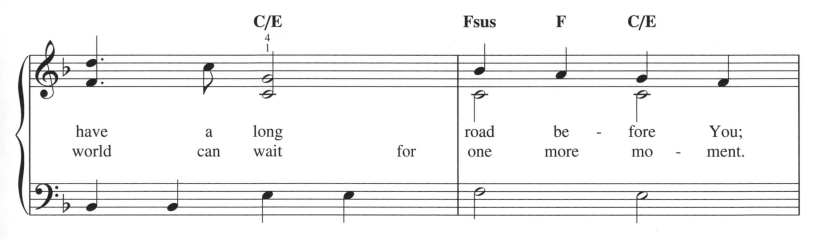

have   a   long   road   be - fore   You;
world   can   wait   for   one   more   mo - ment.

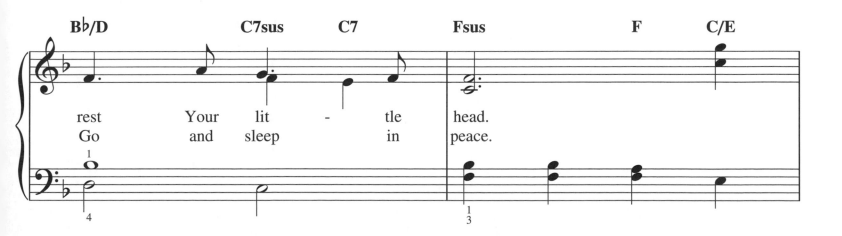

rest   Your   lit - tle   head.
Go   and   sleep   in   peace.

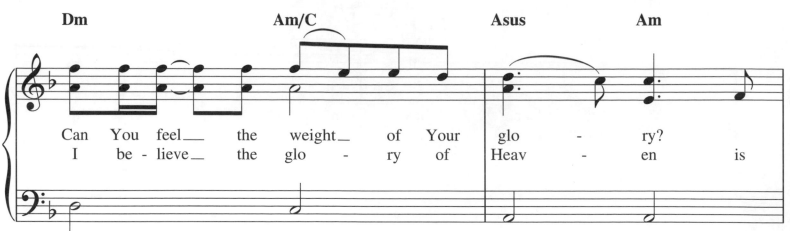

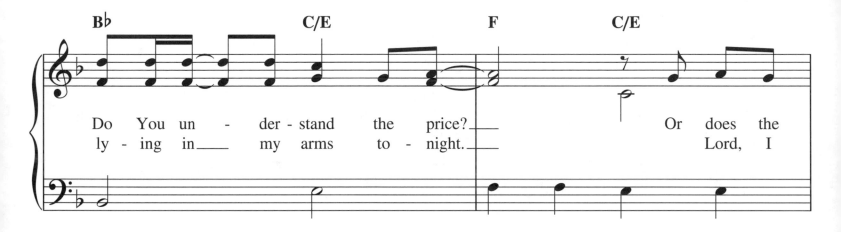

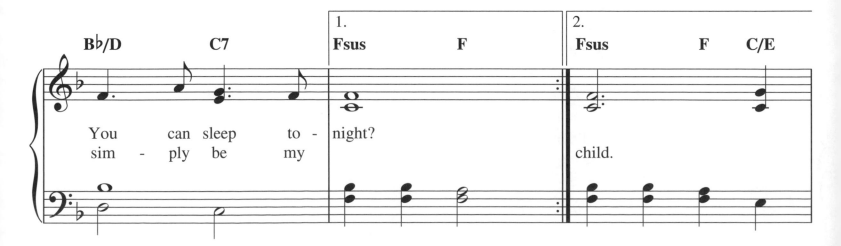

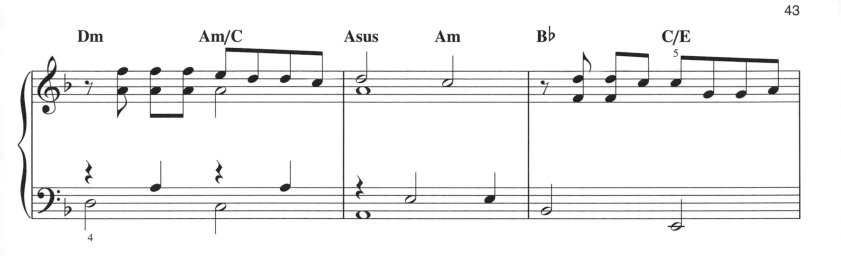

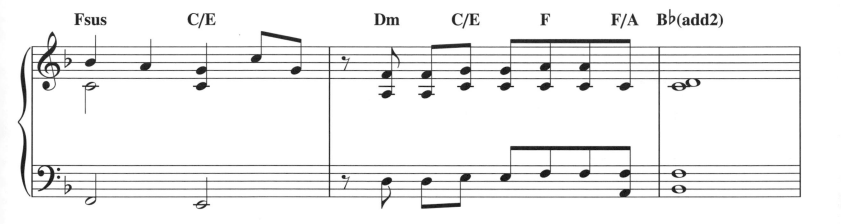

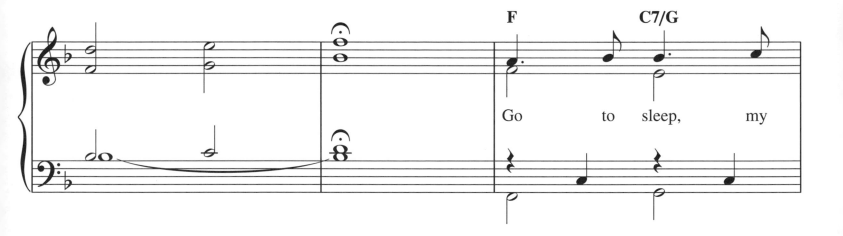

44

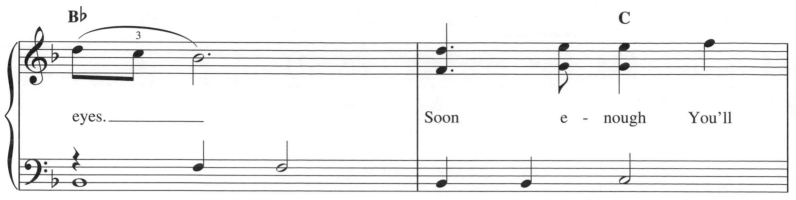

eyes._____ Soon e - nough You'll

save the day, but for now, dear child of

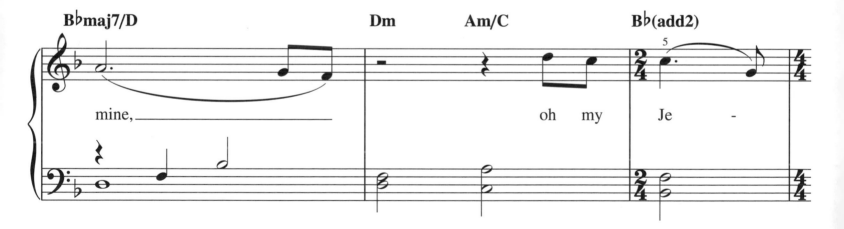

mine,_____ oh my Je -

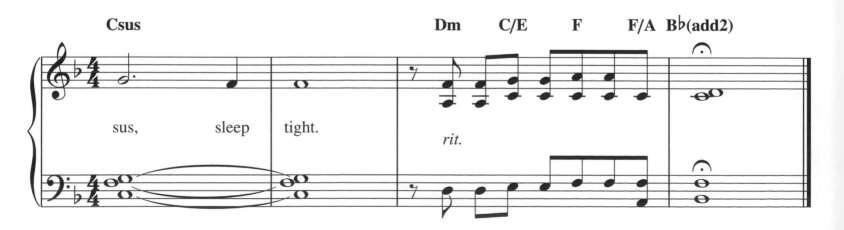

sus, sleep tight. *rit.*

LET THERE BE LIGHT

Words and Music by SCOTT KRIPPAYNE
and MARIE REYNOLDS

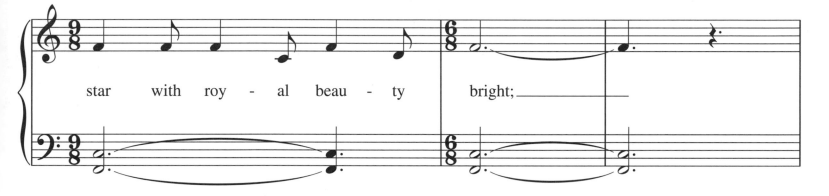

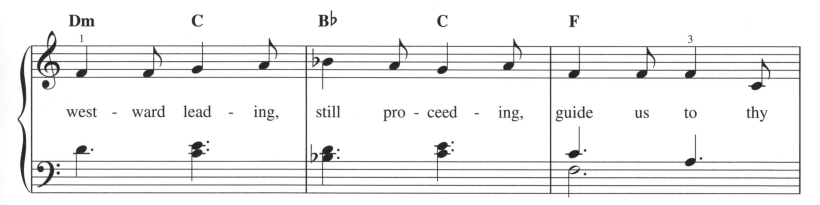

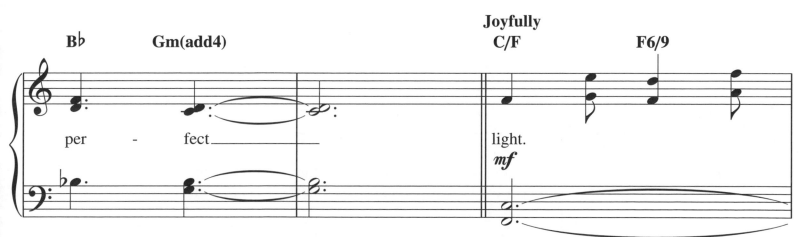

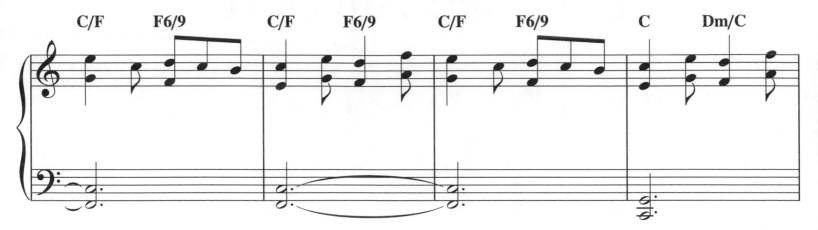

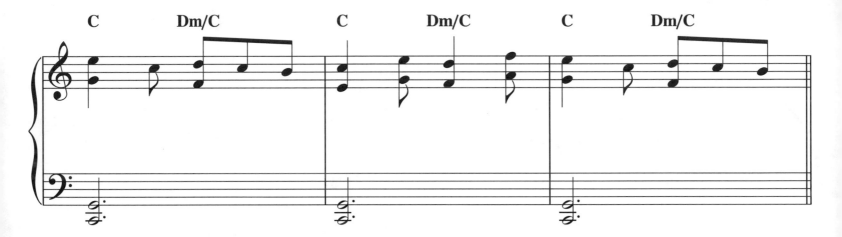

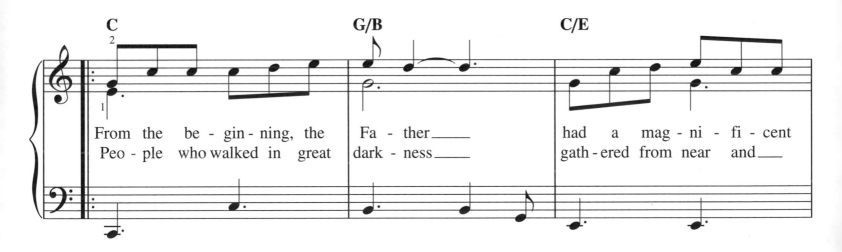

From the be - gin - ning, the | Fa - ther_____ | had a mag - ni - fi - cent
Peo - ple who walked in great | dark - ness_____ | gath - ered from near and___

plan,_____ re- | vealed through the Law and the | proph - ets_____ to ful-
far,_____ | shep - herds with flocks in their | keep - ing,_____

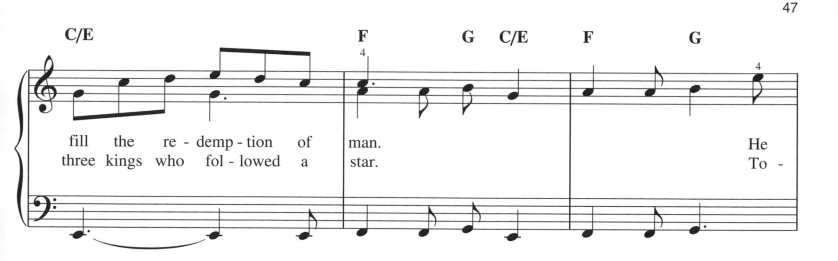

fill the re - demp - tion of | man. | He
three kings who fol - lowed a | star. | To -

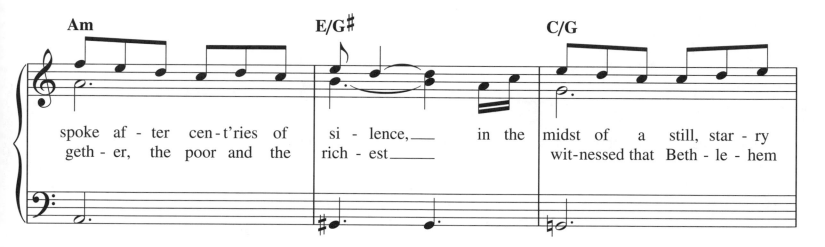

spoke af - ter cen - t'ries of | si - lence,___ in the | midst of a still, star - ry
geth - er, the poor and the | rich - est___ | wit-nessed that Beth - le - hem

night. | And Em - man - u - el came down a - | mong us,___ and the
night, | and the | sky full of an - gels an - | nounc - ing___ the

Fa - ther said, "Let there be | light!" }
birth of the glo - ri - ous | Light. } | Let there be | light, let it shine

48

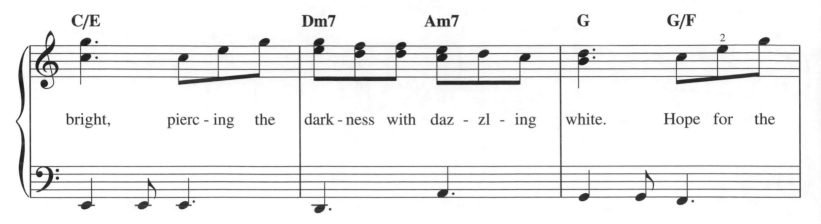

bright, pierc - ing the dark - ness with daz - zl - ing white. Hope for the

hope - less was born on that night, ____ when God sent His Son

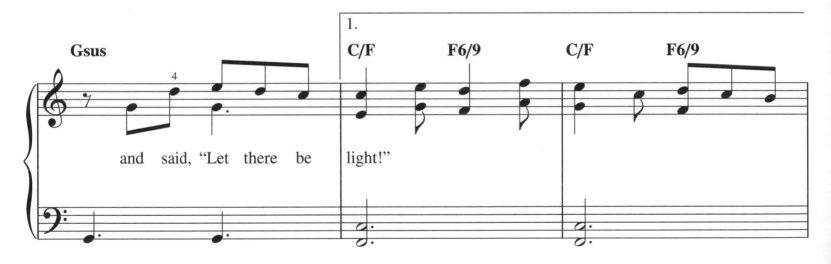

and said, "Let there be light!"

Let there be light!"

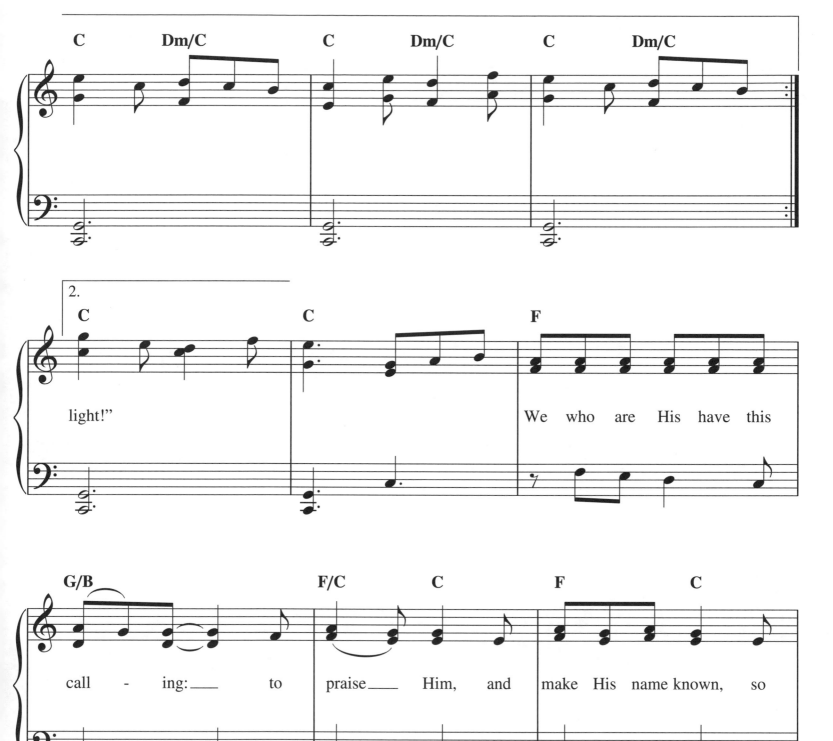

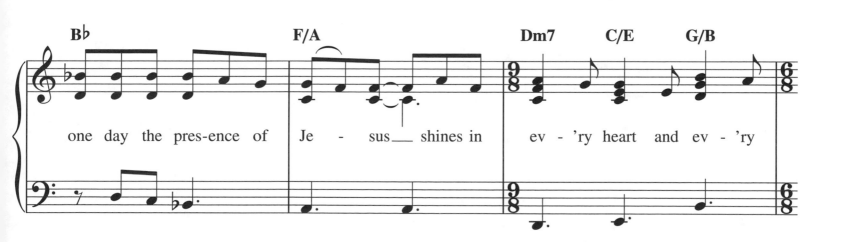

50

A   A/G   D(add2)/F#   D/F#   G(add2)

home,   shines in our

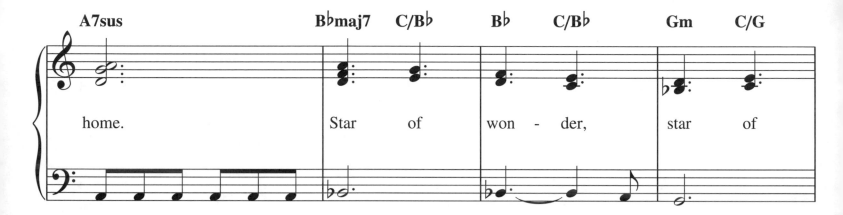

A7sus   Bbmaj7   C/Bb   Bb   C/Bb   Gm   C/G

home.   Star   of   won - der,   star of

Gm7   N.C.   C G/B Am7   G   G/F

beau - ty   bright.____   Let there be light,   let it shine

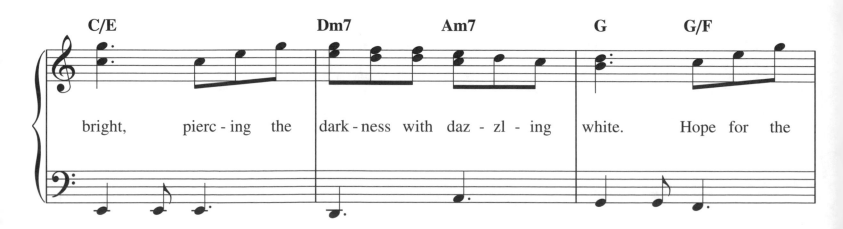

C/E   Dm7   Am7   G   G/F

bright,   pierc-ing the dark-ness with daz-zl-ing white.   Hope for the

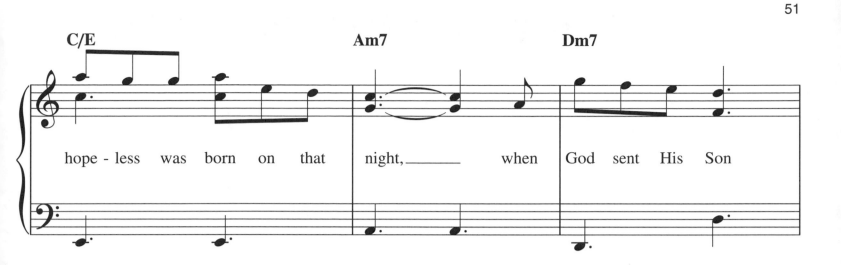

C/E   **Am7**   **Dm7**

hope- less was born on that night,_____ when God sent His Son

1.
Gsus

and said, "Let there be

2.
Gsus   **C**   **Dm/C**

and said, "Let there be light!"

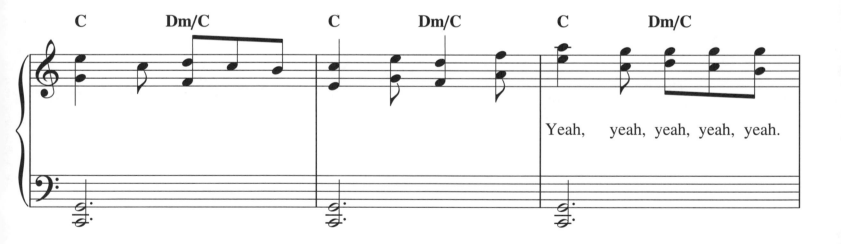

C   **Dm/C**   **C**   **Dm/C**   **C**   **Dm/C**

Yeah,   yeah, yeah, yeah, yeah.

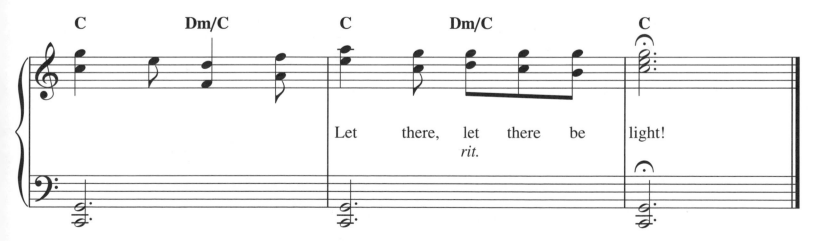

C   **Dm/C**   **C**   **Dm/C**   **C**

Let there, let there be light!
rit.

THE MIRACLE OF CHRISTMAS

Words and Music by
STEVEN CURTIS CHAPMAN

Moderately

A Child is born to-night in Beth-le - hem. His

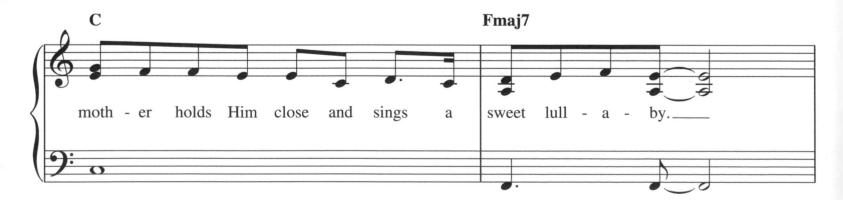

moth - er holds Him close and sings a sweet lull - a - by.____

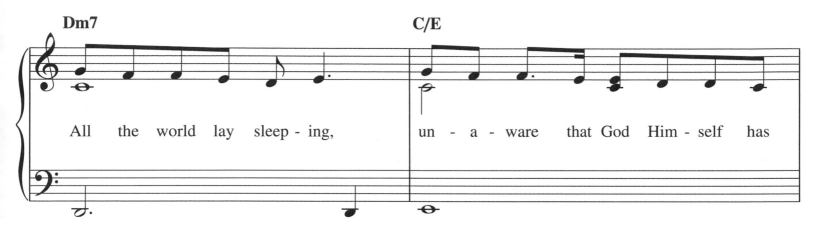

Dm7 / C/E

All the world lay sleep-ing, un-a-ware that God Him-self has

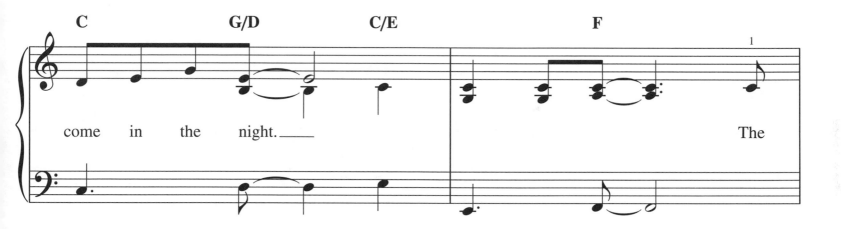

C / G/D / C/E / F

come in the night.____ The

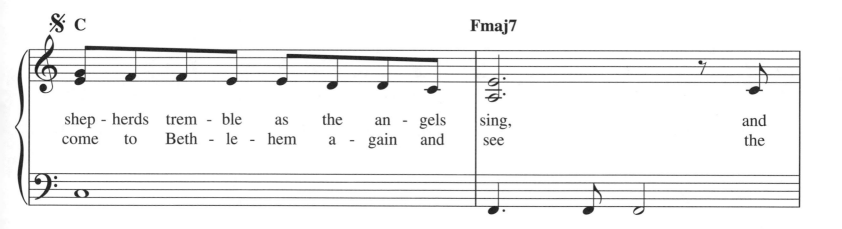

C / Fmaj7

shep-herds trem-ble as the an-gels sing, and
come to Beth-le-hem a-gain and see the

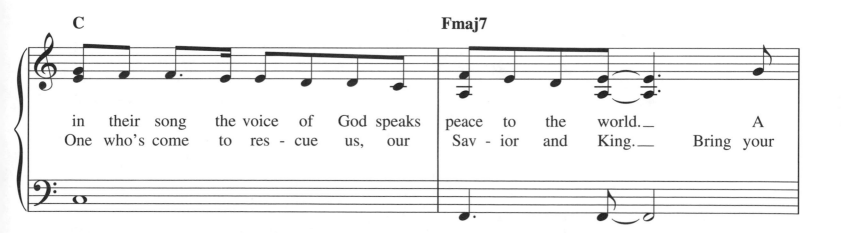

C / Fmaj7

in their song the voice of God speaks peace to the world.__ A
One who's come to res-cue us, our Sav-ior and King.__ Bring your

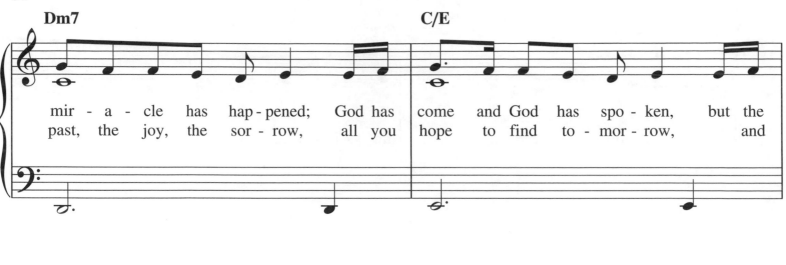

Dm7   **C/E**

mir - a - cle has hap - pened; God has come and God has spo - ken, but the
past, the joy, the sor - row, all you hope to find to - mor - row, and

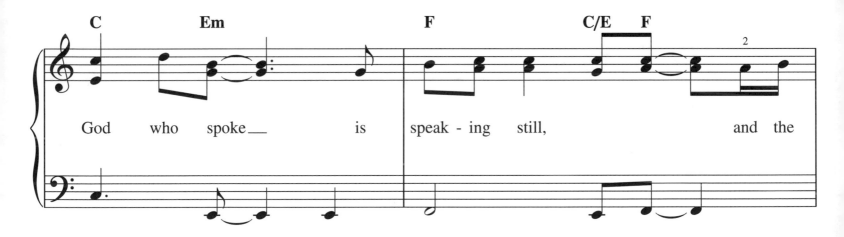

Fsus2

mir - a - cle has on - ly just be - gun. And the
hear the words a - gain, "Fear not," and know that God is near. For the

C   **Em**   **F**   **C/E**   **F**

God who spoke___ is speak - ing still, and the

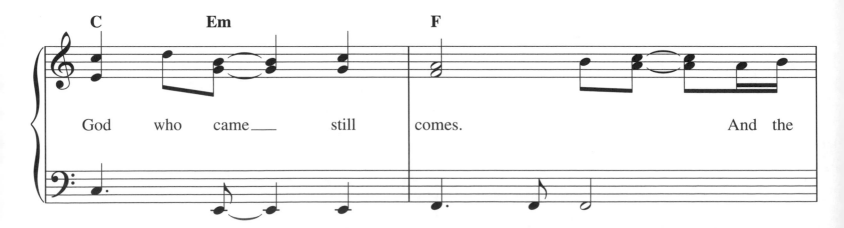

C   **Em**   **F**

God who came___ still comes. And the

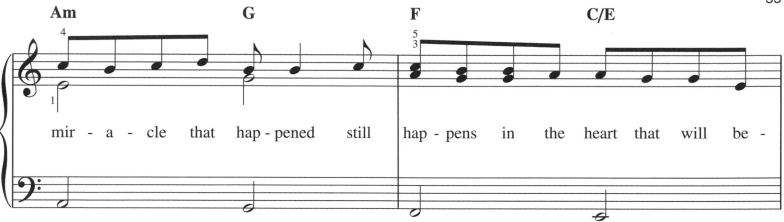

mir - a - cle that hap - pened still | hap - pens in the heart that will be -

lieve   and re - ceive   the mir - a - cle of | Christ - mas.

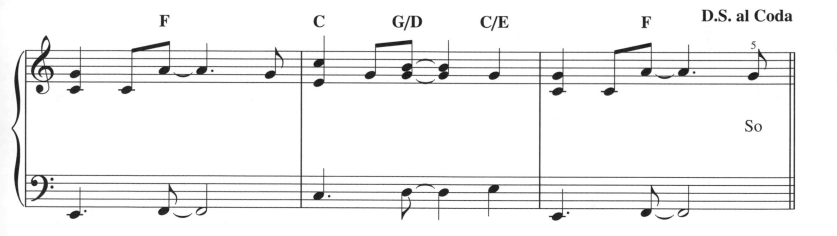

So

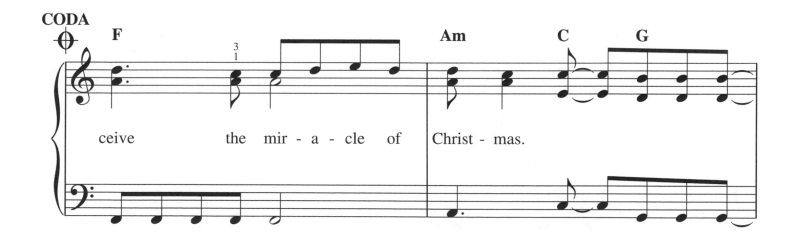

ceive   the mir - a - cle of | Christ - mas.

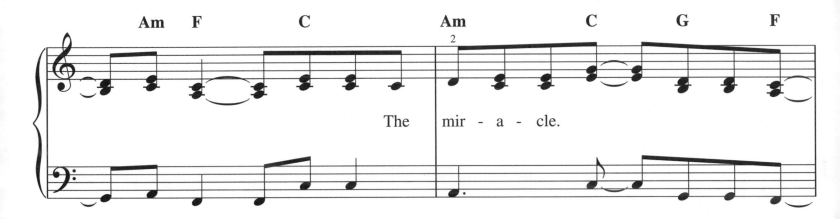

The mir - a - cle.

And the God who spoke_ is speak - ing still, and the

God who came_ still comes. And the mir - a - cle that hap - pened still

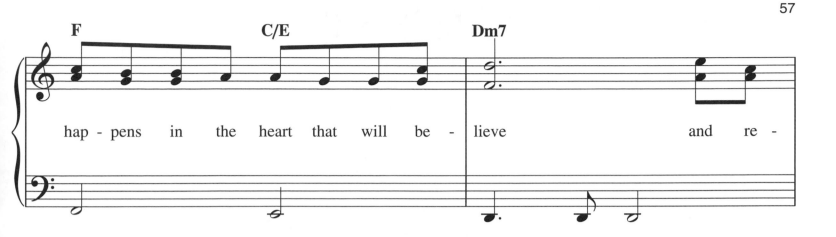

hap - pens in the heart that will be - lieve and re -

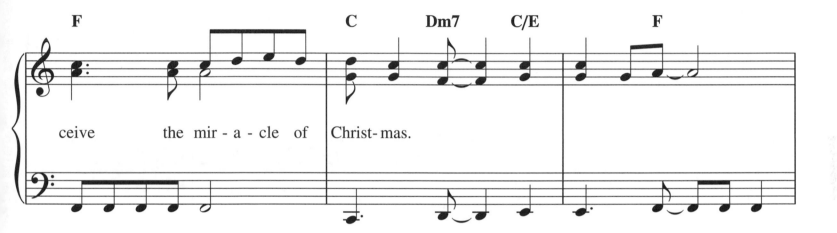

ceive the mir - a - cle of Christ-mas.

Be-lieve the mir - a - cle of Christ-mas.

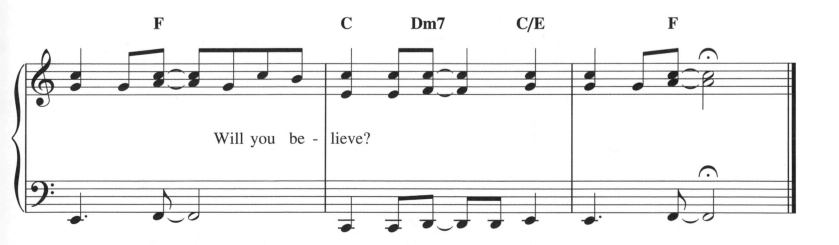

Will you be - lieve?

THIS BABY

Words and Music by
STEVEN CURTIS CHAPMAN

Gently
N.C.

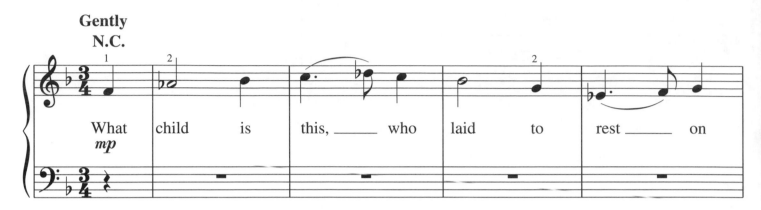

What child is this, _____ who laid to rest _____ on

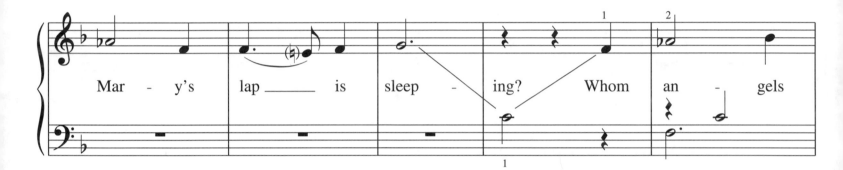

Mar - y's lap _____ is sleep - ing? Whom an - gels

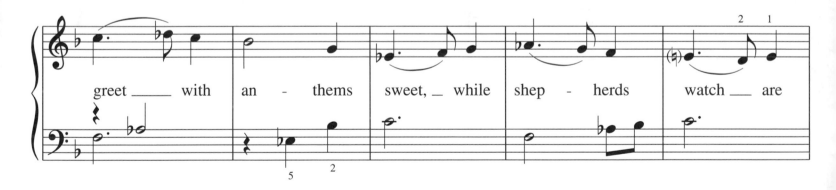

greet _____ with an - thems sweet, _ while shep - herds watch _____ are

Rhythmically
F5

keep - ing?

Well, he

Bb · C · F · Bb · C

cried when he was hun - gry, did all the things that ba - bies
ba - by grew in - to a young boy. He learned to read and write and wres - tle with

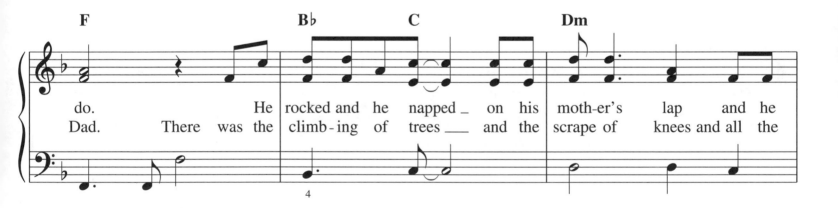

F · Bb · C · Dm

do. He rocked and he napped on his moth - er's lap and he
Dad. There was the climb - ing of trees and the scrape of knees and all the

Bb · C

wig - gled and wig - gled and cooed. There were the cheers when he took his
fun that a boy's born to have. He grew tall - er and some things start - ed

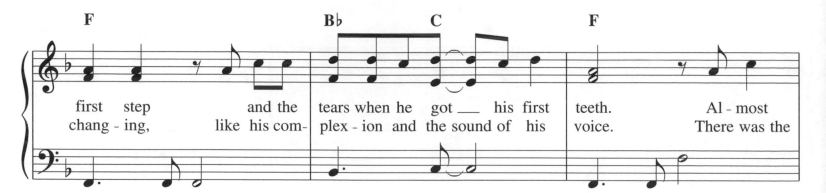

first step   and the | tears when he got ___ his first | teeth.   Al - most
chang - ing,   like his com- | plex - ion and the sound of his | voice.   There was the

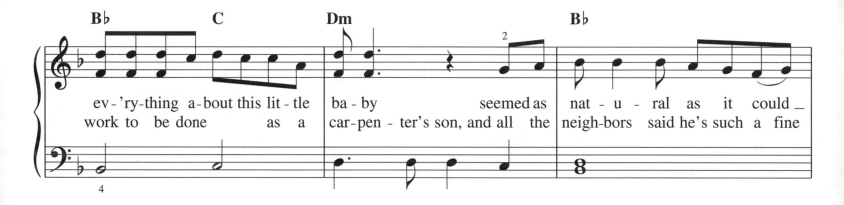

ev - 'ry-thing a-bout this lit - tle | ba - by   seemed as | nat - u - ral as it could ___
work to be done   as a | car-pen - ter's son, and all the | neigh-bors said he's such a fine

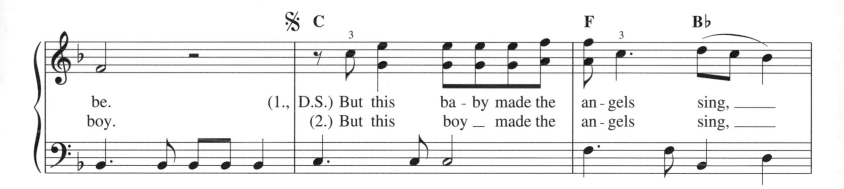

be.   (1., D.S.) But this | ba - by made the | an - gels sing, _____
boy.   (2.) But this | boy __ made the | an - gels sing, _____

and this | ba - by made a | new star shine in the | sky. This | ba - by had
and this | boy __ made a | new star shine in the | sky. This | boy __ had

come   to   change _ the   world. _____   This   ba - by was
come   to   change _ the   world. _____   This   boy __ was

God's own   Son. _____   This   ba - by was   like no __ oth - er one.
God's own   Son. _____   This   boy __ was   like no __ oth - er one.

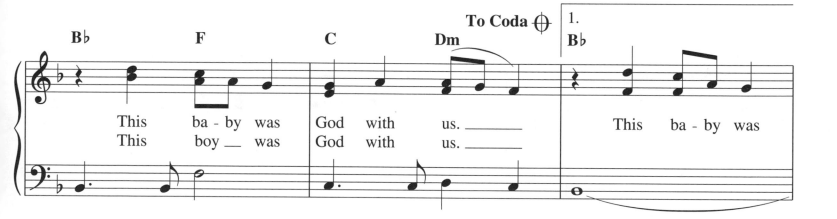

This   ba - by was   God with   us. _____   This   ba - by was
This   boy __ was   God with   us. _____

Je - sus.

And this | This boy __ be - came a __ man. __

Love made Him laugh, _ | death made Him cry, _ but the | life that He lived _ and the

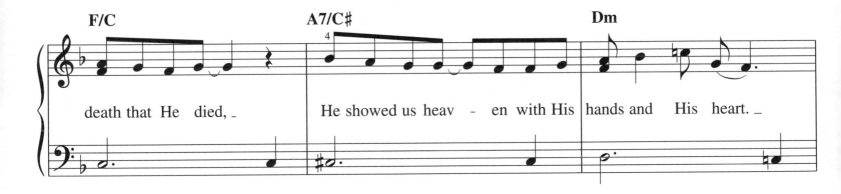

death that He died, _ | He showed us heav - en with His | hands and His heart. _

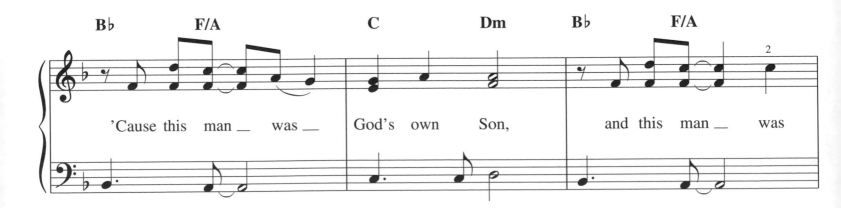

'Cause this man _ was _ | God's own Son, | and this man _ was

63

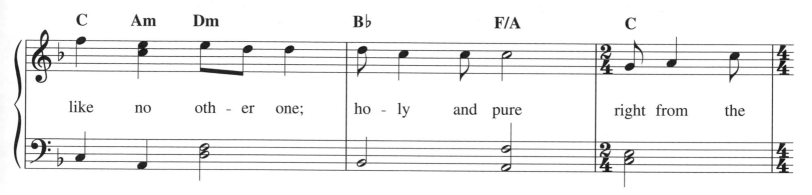

like no oth - er one; ho - ly and pure right from the

start, yeah, yeah.

This ba - by,

this ba - by was Je - sus.

This ba - by was Je - sus.

WELCOME TO OUR WORLD

Words and Music by
CHRIS RICE

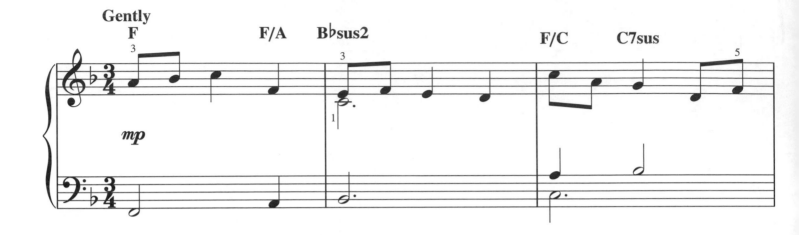

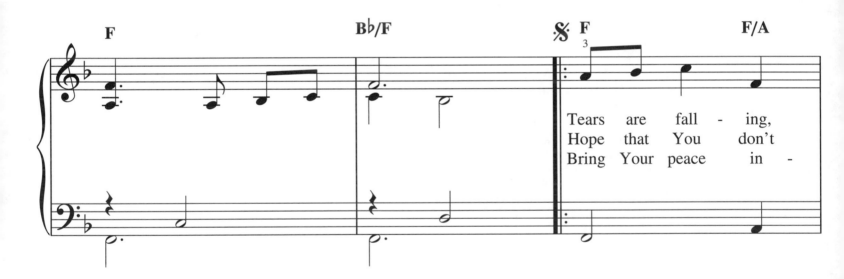

Tears are fall - ing,
Hope that You don't
Bring Your peace in -

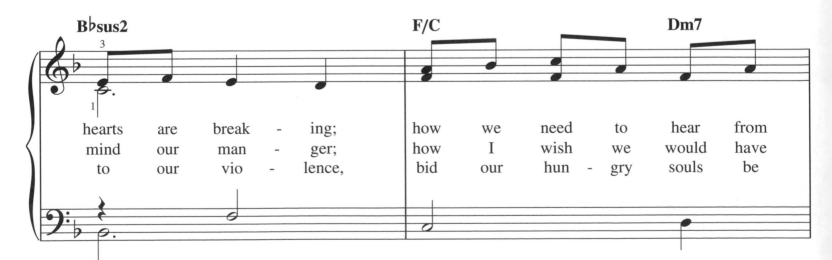

hearts are break - ing;
mind our man - ger;
to our vio - lence,

how we need to hear from
how I wish we would have
bid our hun - gry souls be

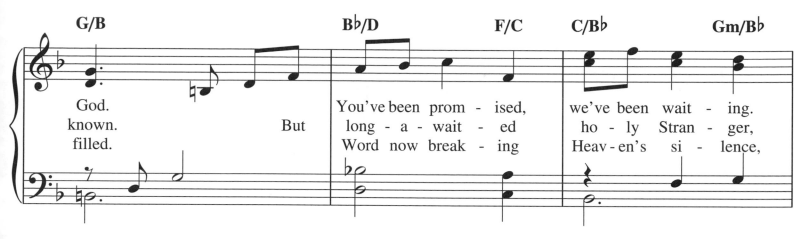

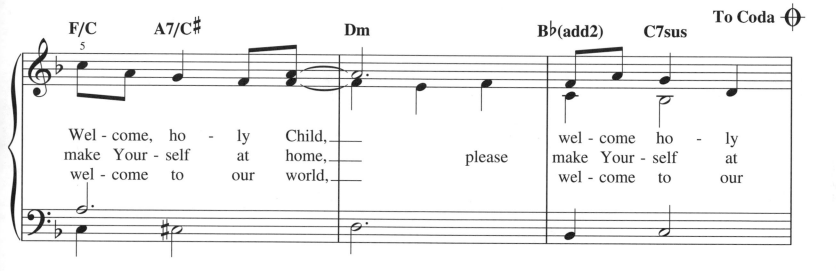

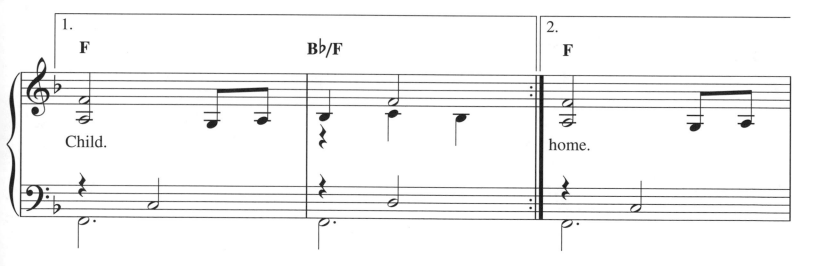

CODA

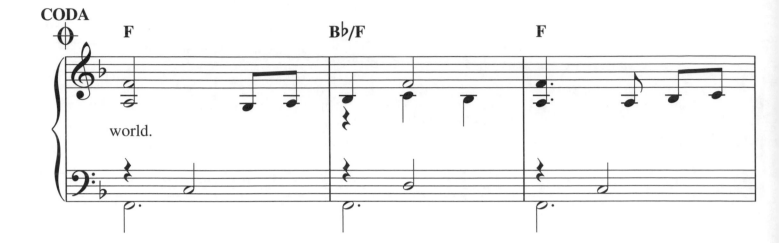

world.

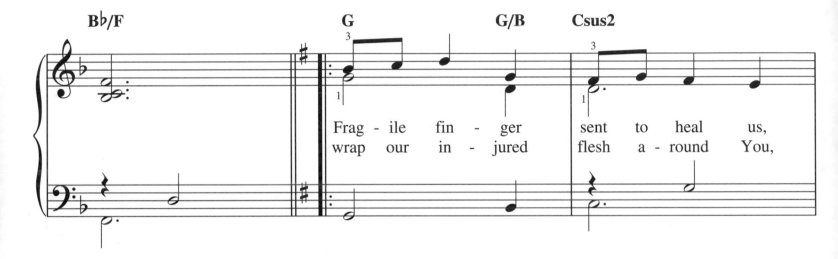

Frag - ile fin - ger sent to heal us,
wrap our in - jured flesh a - round You,

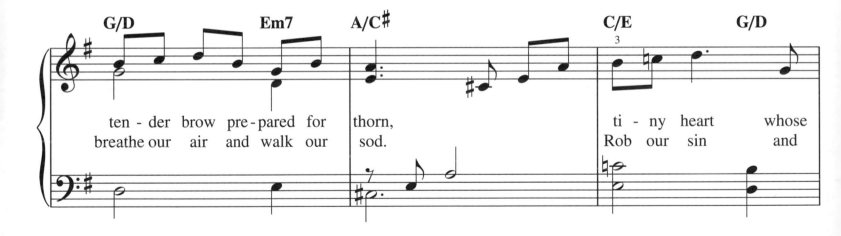

ten - der brow pre-pared for thorn, ti - ny heart whose
breathe our air and walk our sod. Rob our sin and

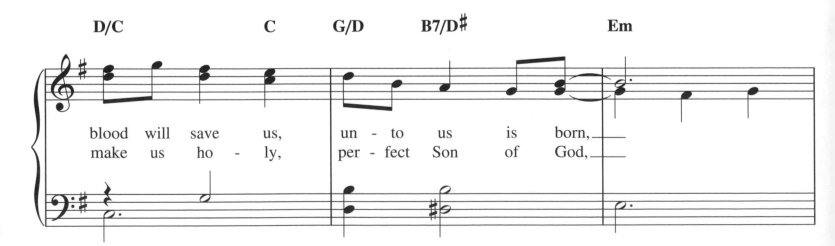

blood will save us, un - to us is born,___
make us ho - ly, per - fect Son of God,___

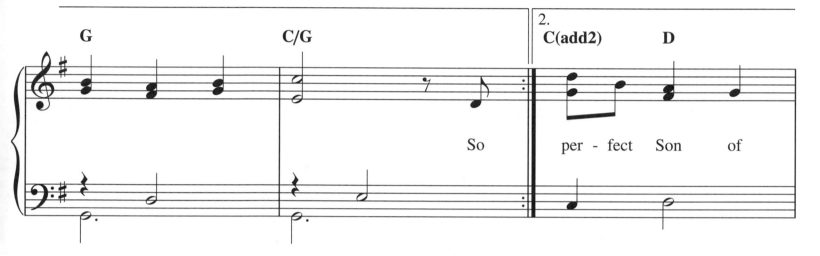

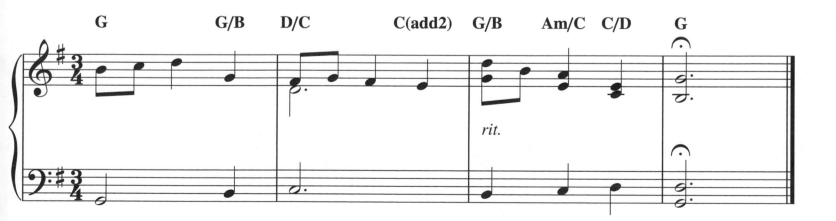

A STRANGE WAY TO SAVE THE WORLD

Words and Music by DAVE CLARK,
MARK HARRIS and DON KOCH

I'm sure he must have been sur - prised

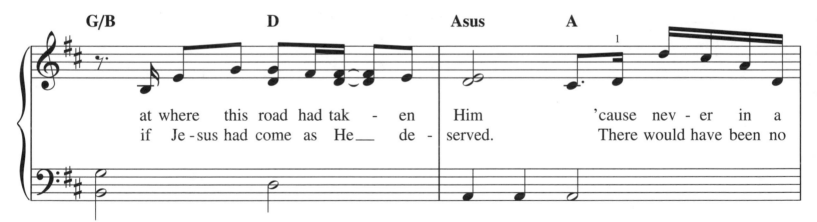

at where this road had tak - en Him 'cause nev - er in a
if Je - sus had come as He_ de - served. There would have been no

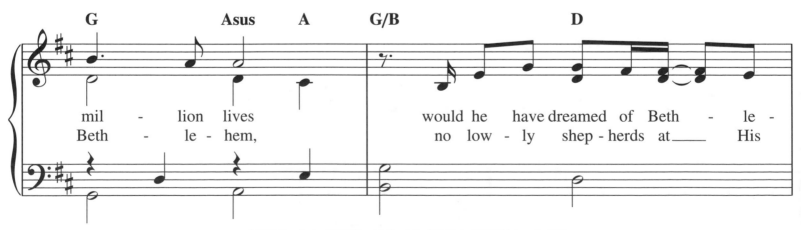

mil - lion lives
Beth - le - hem, would he have dreamed of Beth - le -
no low - ly shep - herds at_ His

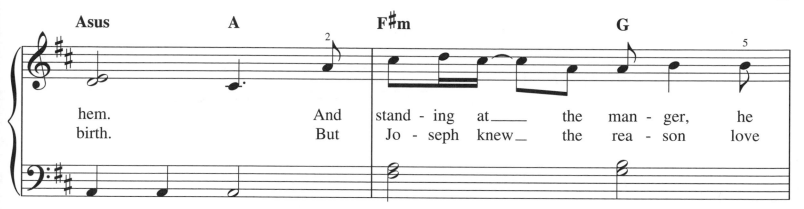

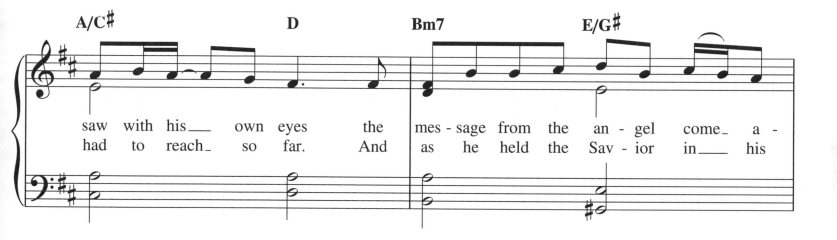

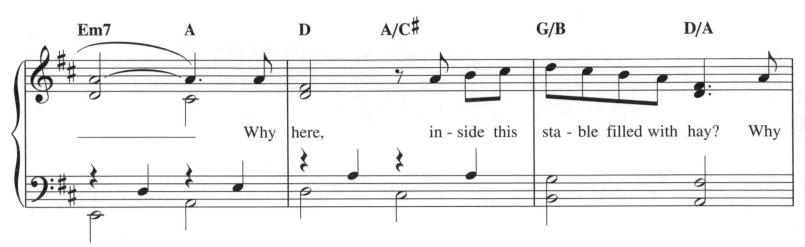

Why here, in - side this sta - ble filled with hay? Why

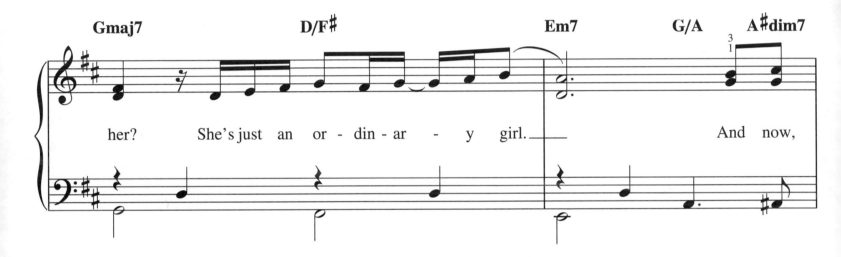

her? She's just an or - din - ar - y girl. And now,

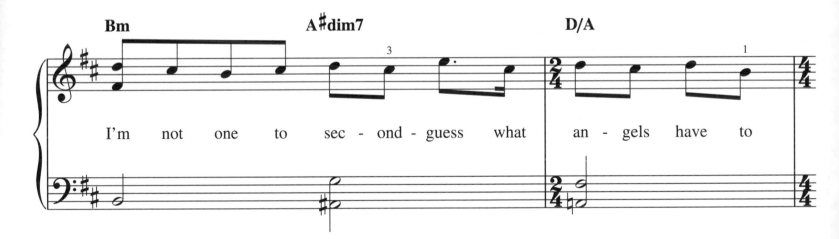

I'm not one to sec - ond - guess what an - gels have to

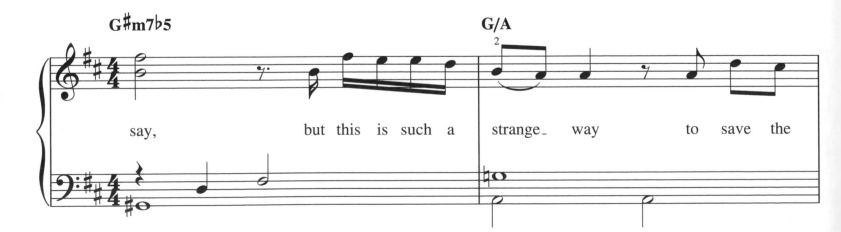

say, but this is such a strange way to save the

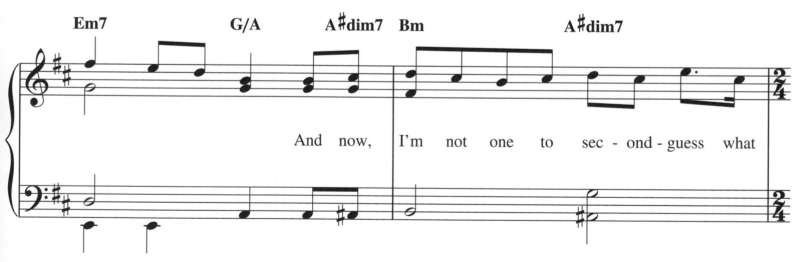

strange_ way   to save the   world.   This is such a

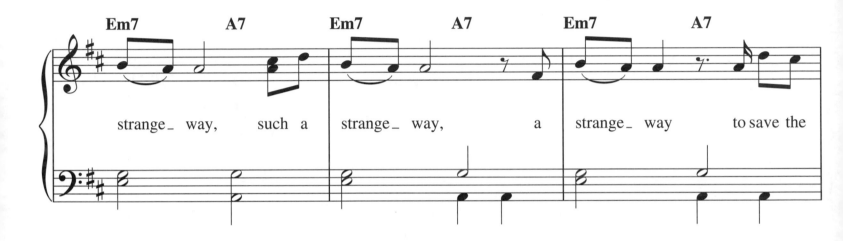

strange_ way,   such a   strange_ way,   a   strange_ way   to save the

world.____   Whoa,____   whoa,__   whoa.

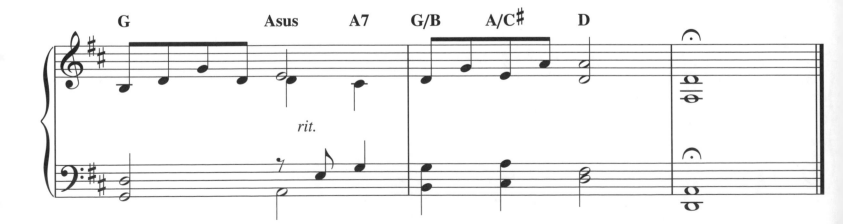

rit.

WHILE YOU WERE SLEEPING

Words and Music by
MARK HALL

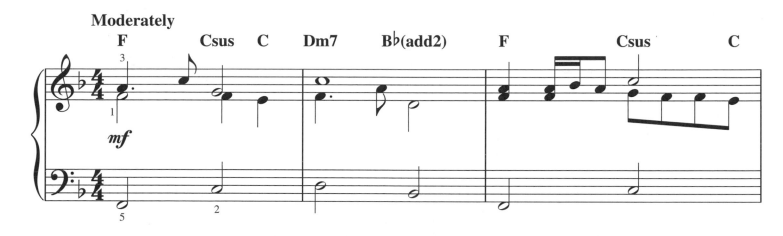

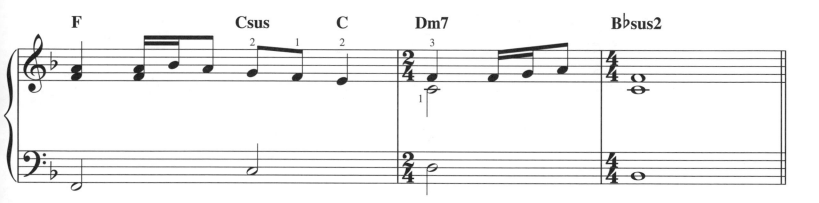

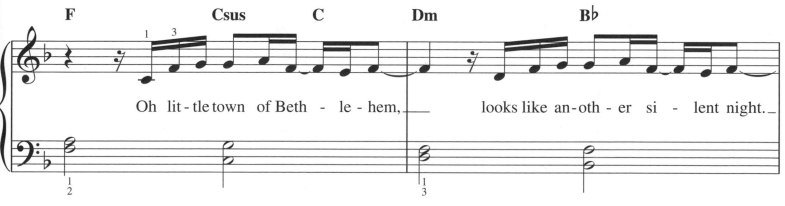

Oh lit - tle town of Beth - le - hem,___ looks like an - oth - er si - lent night.___

A-bove your deep and dream-less

sleep, a gi - ant star lights up the sky._____

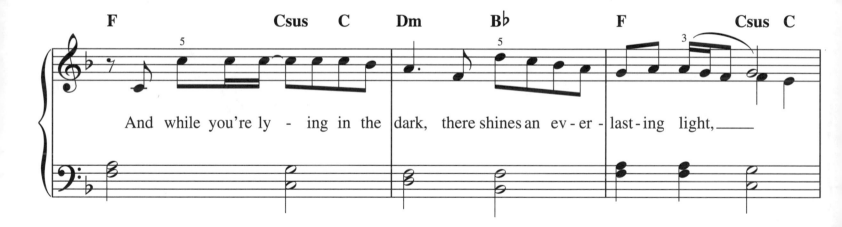

And while you're ly - ing in the dark, there shines an ev - er - last-ing light,_____

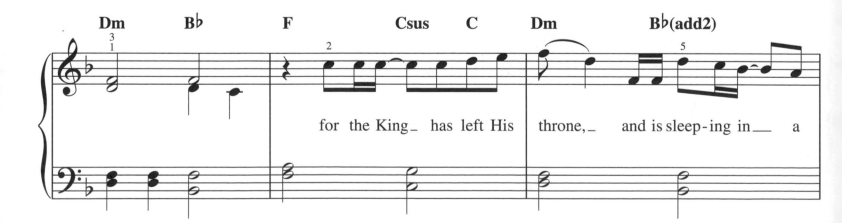

for the King_ has left His throne,_ and is sleep-ing in _ a

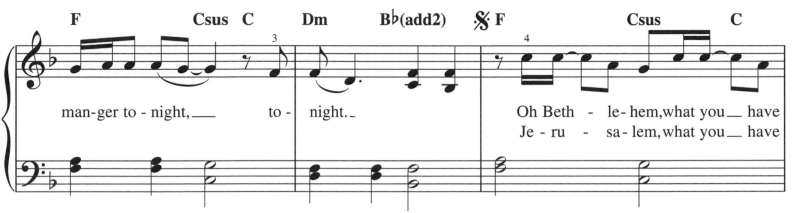

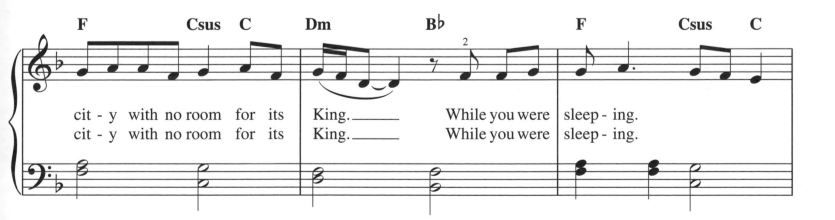

While you were | sleep - ing.
While you were | sleep - ing.

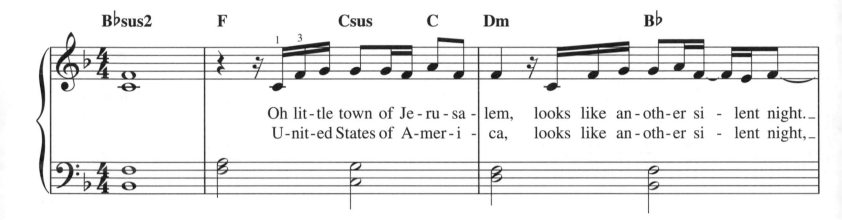

Oh lit - tle town of Je - ru - sa - lem, looks like an - oth - er si - lent night.
U - nit - ed States of A - mer - i - ca, looks like an - oth - er si - lent night,

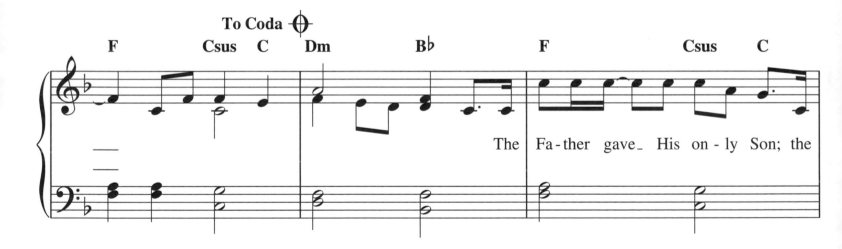

The | Fa - ther gave His on - ly Son; the

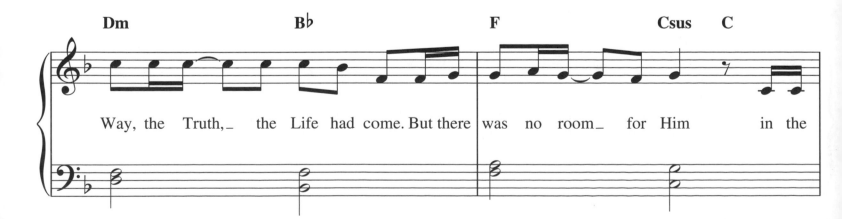

Way, the Truth, the Life had come. But there | was no room for Him in the

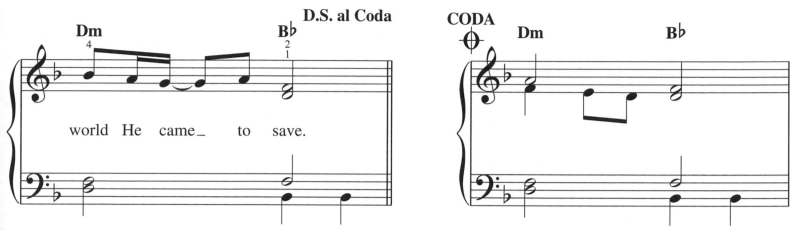

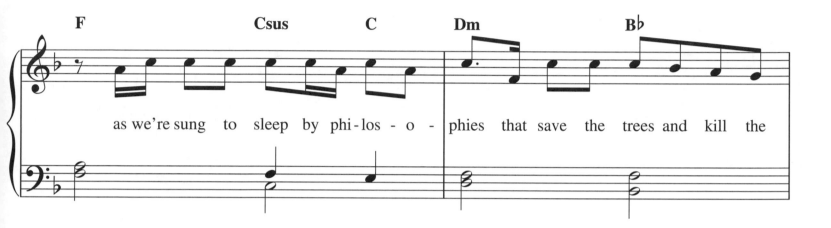

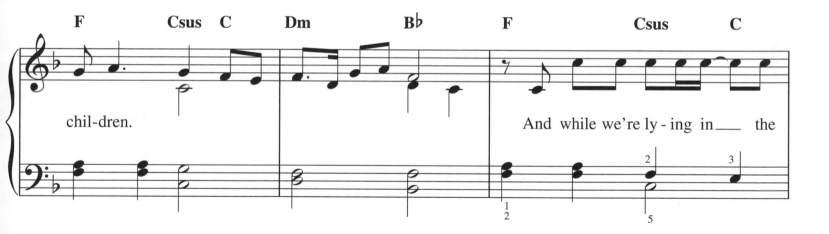

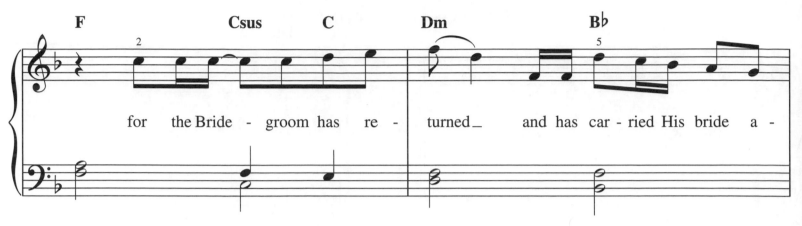

for the Bride - groom has re - turned__ and has car - ried His bride a -

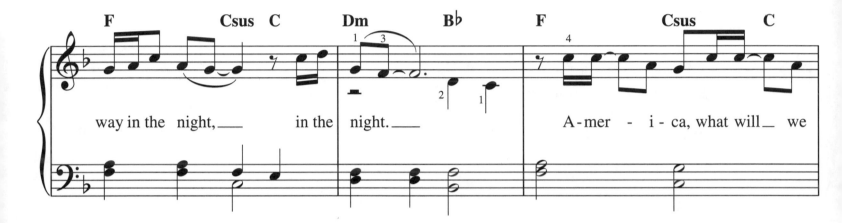

way in the night,___ in the night.___ A - mer - i - ca, what will__ we

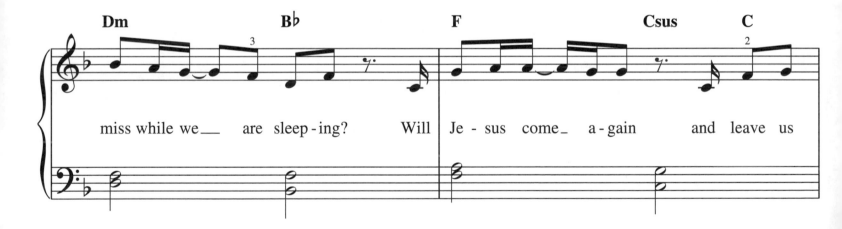

miss while we__ are sleep - ing? Will Je - sus come__ a - gain and leave us

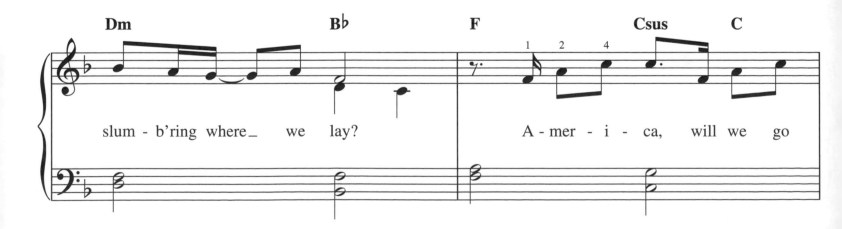

slum - b'ring where__ we lay? A - mer - i - ca, will we go

down_ in his-to-ry___ as a na-tion with no room for its King?___ Willwe be

sleep-ing? Will we be sleep-ing?

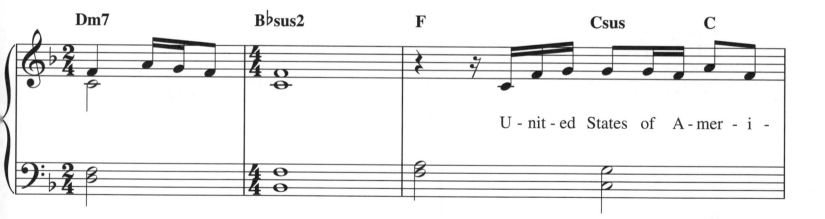

U - nit - ed States of A - mer - i -

ca, looks like an-oth-er si - lent night. *rit.*

More Contemporary Christian Folios from Hal Leonard

Arranged for Piano, Voice and Guitar

THE VERY BEST OF AVALON – TESTIFY TO LOVE

All 16 songs from the 2003 compilation by this acclaimed vocal quartet: Adonai • Can't Live a Day • Don't Save It All for Christmas Day • Everything to Me • Give It Up • Knockin' on Heaven's Door • New Day • Pray • Testify to Love • and more.
00306526 ....$16.95

JEREMY CAMP – RESTORED

All 12 tracks from the 2004 release: Be the One • Breathe • Even When • Everytime • Innocence • Lay Down My Pride • Letting Go • My Desire • Nothing Else I Need • Restored • Take You Back • This Man.
00306701 ....$16.95

CASTING CROWNS – LIFESONG

11 contemporary rock/worship songs from this popular band's 2005 album. Includes: And Now My Lifesong Sings • Does Anybody Hear Her • Father, Spirit, Jesus • In Me • Lifesong • Love Them like Jesus • Praise You in This Storm • Prodigal • Set Me Free • Stained Glass Masquerade • While You Were Sleeping.
00306748 ....$16.95

STEVEN CURTIS CHAPMAN – ALL THINGS NEW

Matching folio to the latest release from this perennial CCM favorite and multi-Dove Award winner. 12 songs, including: All Things New • Angels Wish • Believe Me Now • The Big Story • Coming Attractions • I Believe in You • Last Day on Earth • Much of You • Only Getting Started • Please Only You • Treasure of Jesus • What Now.
00306662 ....$14.95

THE DAVID CROWDER*BAND COLLECTION

Based in Waco, Texas, David Crowder's innovative alt-pop style has made him one of today's most popular worship leaders. This collection includes 16 of his best songs: Here Is Our King • No One like You • Open Skies • Our Love Is Loud • You Alone • and more.
00306776 ....$16.95

For More Information, See Your Local Music Dealer, Or Write To:

HAL•LEONARD® CORPORATION

7777 W. Bluemound Rd. P.O. Box 13819 Milwaukee, WI 53213

For a complete listing of the products we have available, Visit us online at **www.halleonard.com**

DC TALK – INTERMISSION: THE GREATEST HITS

17 of DC Talk's best: Between You and Me • Chance • Colored People • Consume Me • Hardway (Remix) • I Wish We'd All Been Ready • In the Light • Jesus Freak • Jesus Is Just Alright • Luv Is a Verb • Mind's Eye • My Will • Say the Words • Socially Acceptable • SugarCoat It • Supernatural • What If I Stumble.
00306414 ....$14.95

BETHANY DILLON – IMAGINATION

16-year-old singer/songwriter/ guitarist Bethany Dillon shows depth and talent beyond her years in this 2005 sophomore release. Includes 11 songs: Airplane • All That I Can Do • Be Near Me • Dreamer • Hallelujah • I Believe in You • Imagination • My Love Hasn't Grown Cold • New • Vagabond • The Way I See You.
00306745 ....$16.95

JENNIFER KNAPP – THE COLLECTION

15 songs from Knapp's greatest hits collection: Breathe on Me • By and By • Diamond in the Rough • Hold Me Now • Into You • Lay It Down • A Little More • Martyrs & Thieves • Refine Me • Romans • Say Won't You Say • Undo Me • The Way I Am • When Nothing Satisfies • Whole Again.
00306623 ....$14.95

KUTLESS – STRONG TOWER

The 2005 release by this Christian hard rock band hailing from Oregon includes 13 tracks: We Fall Down • Take Me In • Ready for You • Draw Me Close • Better Is One Day • I Lift My Eyes Up • Word of God Speak • Arms of Love • and more.
00306726 ....$16.95

Music Inspired by
THE CHRONICLES OF NARNIA

The Lion, The Witch and the Wardrobe 11 songs from the album featuring CCM artists performing songs inspired by the book and movie. Includes: I Will Believe (Nichole Nordeman) • Lion (Rebecca St. James) • Remembering You (Steven Curtis Chapman) • Waiting for the World to Fall (Jars of Clay) • and more.
00313311 ....$16.95

NEWSBOYS – DEVOTION

All 10 tracks from the 2004 recording by these alt CCM rockers: Blessed Be Your Name • Devotion • God of Nations • I Love Your Ways • Landslide of Love • Name Above All Names • The Orphan • Presence • Strong Tower • When the Tears Fall.
00306702 ....$16.95

NICHOLE NORDEMAN – BRAVE

11 tracks from the 2005 album by this talented singer-songwriter: Brave • Crimson • Gotta Serve Somebody • Hold On • Lay It Down • Live • No More Chains • Real to Me • Someday • We Build • What If.
00306729 ....$16.95

TWILA PARIS – HOUSE OF WORSHIP

Includes 12 songs: Christ in Us • Come Emmanuel • Fill My Heart • For Eternity • Glory and Honor • God of All • I Want the World to Know • Make Us One • Not My Own • We Bow Down • We Will Glorify • You Are God.
00306517 ....$14.95

PHILLIPS, CRAIG AND DEAN – LET YOUR GLORY FALL

10 songs from the 2003 release: Every Day • Fall Down • Hallelujah • Here I Am to Worship • How Deep the Father's Love for Us • Let Your Glory Fall • My Praise • Only You • What Kind of Love Is This • The Wonderful Cross.
00306519 ....$14.95

REBECCA ST. JAMES – IF I HAD ONE CHANCE TO TELL YOU SOMETHING

All 12 songs from this Aussie artist's 2005 album: Alive • Beautiful Stranger • Forgive Me • God Help Me • I Can Trust You • I Need You • Lest I Forget • Love Being Loved By You • Shadowlands • Take All of Me • Thank You • You Are Loved.
00306770 ....$16.95

SWITCHFOOT – NOTHING IS SOUND

Switchfoot's rock style and street-smart faith has given them widespread success in CCM and secular arenas. This songbook from their 2005 release features 12 songs: Daisy • Happy Is a Yuppie Word • Lonely Nation • The Setting Sun • Stars • more.
00306756 ....$16.95

THIRD DAY – WHEREVER YOU ARE

This popular rock band's 2005 release features "Cry Out to Jesus" plus: Carry My Cross • Communion • Eagles • How Do You Know • I Can Feel It • Keep on Shinin' • Love Heals Your Heart • Mountain of God • Rise Up • The Sun Is Shining • Tunnel.
00306766 ....$16.95

1205